MIND
POWER

MIND
POWER

Secret Strategies for the Martial Arts

KAZUMI TABATA
Foreword by Kaiichi Hasumi

TUTTLE Publishing
Tokyo | Rutland, Vermont | Singapore

"Books to Span the East and West"

Tuttle Publishing was founded in 1832 in the small New England town of Rutland, Vermont [USA]. Our core values remain as strong today as they were then—to publish best-in-class books which bring people together one page at a time. In 1948, we established a publishing office in Japan—and Tuttle is now a leader in publishing English-language books about the arts, languages and cultures of Asia. The world has become a much smaller place today and Asia's economic and cultural influence has grown. Yet the need for meaningful dialogue and information about this diverse region has never been greater. Over the past seven decades, Tuttle has published thousands of books on subjects ranging from martial arts and paper crafts to language learning and literature—and our talented authors, illustrators, designers and photographers have won many prestigious awards. We welcome you to explore the wealth of information available on Asia at **www.tuttlepublishing.com**.

Please note that the publisher and author(s) of this instructional book are NOT RESPONSIBLE in any manner whatsoever for any injury that may result from practicing the techniques and/or following the instructions given within. Martial arts training can be dangerous—both to you and to others—if not practiced safely. If you're in doubt as to how to proceed or whether your practice is safe, consult with a trained martial arts teacher before beginning. Since the physical activities described herein may be too strenuous in nature for some readers, it is also essential that a physician be consulted prior to training.

Published by Tuttle Publishing, an imprint of Periplus Editions (HK) Ltd.

www.tuttlepublishing.com

First edition

25 24 23 22
10 9 8 7 6
Printed in China   2211CM

Library of Congress Cataloging-in-Publication Da
Tabata, Kazumi, 1943-
  Mind power : secret strategies for the martial arts
Kazumi Tabata ; foreword by Kaiichi Hasumi.
    158 p. ; 20 cm.
  ISBN 978-0-8048-4109-2 (hardcover)
1. Martial arts--Psychological aspects. 2. Martial
arts--Philosophy. I. Title.
  GV1102.7.P75T33 2010
  796.801'9--dc22
                                        2010010852
ISBN 978-0-8048-4109-2

Distributed by

North America, Latin America & Europe
Tuttle Publishing
364 Innovation Drive
North Clarendon, VT 05759-9436 U.S.A.
Tel: 1 (802) 773-8930; Fax: 1 (802) 773-6993
info@tuttlepublishing.com
www.tuttlepublishing.com

Japan
Tuttle Publishing
Yaekari Building, 3rd Floor; 5-4-12 Osaki
Shinagawa-ku, Tokyo 141 0032
Tel: (81) 3 5437-0171; Fax: (81) 3 5437-0755
sales@tuttle.co.jp
www.tuttle.co.jp

Asia Pacific
Berkeley Books Pte. Ltd.
3 Kallang Sector #04-01, Singapore 349278
Tel: (65) 6741 2178 Fax: (65) 6741 2179
inquiries@periplus.com.sg
www.tuttlepublishing.com

Contents

Foreword

The knowledge inherited from the long history of Asia is compiled in this book as a collection of thoughts. This is an extremely unique book in that it expresses the form and shape of the fighting psyche and spirit through martial arts. I have never before encountered such a finely distilled book. While perusing the book, I felt I could almost touch the core of life. It is an honor for me to encounter this book and I wish to recommend it to as many people as possible. This book also revives the old classics to modernity and is a guidebook to the art of living. I believe it speaks to people from all walks of life and could serve as a good reference. Originator and teacher Kazumi Tabata is one who has been investigating the space and Zen of Karate.

Karate is a way of learning truth. The traditional skill and the truth hidden in the word "Karate" are gleaned from training. When researched using perspectives from sports psychology, religion, meditation, breathing techniques, and personal viewpoints, the way of truth is opened. This part certainly is not glossed over in the book. This book is not just about Karate, but presents a unique worldview that surpasses Karate.

Shihan Tabata trained in the Shotokan style in the Karate Club of Waseda University. After graduation, he studied under Hisao Obata (a leading student of Gichin Funakoshi) who was then at Keio Private University and was the first Chief Director of the Japan Karatedo Federation. The study of "do" in "Karatedo" and the approaches and interpretations initiated by Obata are included within this book.

Shihan Tabata was the first instructor dispatched to the U.S. in 1967, before a system for sending instructors overseas had been initiated by the Japan Karatedo Federation. He has been teaching Karatedo in various countries with a base in Boston. His excellent leadership and instruction, coupled with his broad-minded and cheerful disposition, have led him to mix and integrate well with people and communities in every country. He has been playing an active role as an international goodwill ambassador, in addition to teaching Karatedo.

We has a close friend of the late Dr. Takaichi Mano, the former Chief Director of the Japan Karatedo Federation, and served as an advisor when Dr. Mano took office as the General Secretary of the World Karate Federation.

After he was dispatched to the U.S., Shihan Tabata did not slow down the pace of his own study, but continued the in-depth research of etiquette, Okinawan Kobudo, and Zen, which makes profound his martial arts techniques and spirit.

I hold in high regard the content and passion of this publication. I sincerely hope this book will lead to the development and growth of its readers.

September 2007
Kaiichi Hasumi
Vice President and General Secretary
Japan Karatedo Federation

Preface

There are essentially two paths to enlightenment. One path is art and the other path is religion. The two paths are closely interrelated.

In terms of the martial arts, there are two training methods: one focuses on the rational aspect of training while the other emphasizes the technical aspect. The martial arts owe its origin to people's attempts to rationally unify the mind, body, and skill. In the martial arts, truth will reveal itself once your mind gains insight into the empty nature of the world and your body masters and perfects physical techniques.

Unable to escape from life's suffering, we continually strive to eliminate suffering. The existence of desire and hardship make our lives more worthwhile. Tantalizing clues can be found in nature, which holds the key to overcoming difficulties we encounter in our lives as well as in the martial arts. Those who manage to decipher such clues will eventually transcend their earthly desires and attain enlightenment.

I would be honored if this book could be of any help to you in uncovering the clues to understanding the essence of reality. This book, a sequel to my first book, *Secret Tactics*, is based on my own experience and draws largely on the writings of our predecessors. I recommend reading my first book before proceeding to this book. Further volumes are in preparation.

Gassho
Kazumi Tabata

BOOK ONE

STRATEGY

CHAPTER 1

Strength and Rhythm

Strength and rhythm are essential in *budo* (the martial arts).

Strength and rhythm are also essential in breathing, speed, force, and technique.

One who understands strength and rhythm controls others.

One who does not understand strength and rhythm is controlled by others.

Strength is the result of self-confidence.

Everything in this world has rhythm and so does life.

Rhythm opens one's eyes to reveal the opponent's movement.

One cannot win when the rhythm of one's stroke is agreeable to the adversary's stroke.

If one attacks with opposite rhythm, it will lead to an easy victory.

Obtaining rhythm depends on the quality and quantity of practice.

In order to win one should use unrhythmic strokes. One needs to train to understand and gain force and timing to attack.

Sen-ryaku

KNOWLEDGE OF MIND

Mind and technique correspond to each other.
When one's body is active, the mind is at peace.
When one's body is at peace, the mind is active.
Keeping physical and spiritual balance is fundamental in a fight.

One should acquire a clear and finely-honed mind to be able to hear the sound of wind and water.

When one is equipped with hard-and-fast courage and technique, one can show a flow of technique to correspond with complete control.

There should not be any doubts in technique.

One must have super-brave courage and willpower to overcome life and death in equanimity.

On the battlefield, one should not think whether the adversary is a saint or not.

One must ignore and disregard such thoughts to avoid lowering one's guard and giving a momentary change in mind and attitude.

Temporary victory is meaningless.

Victory for a lifetime is the true victory.

By getting rid of one's self-interest, everything will be in perfect freedom.

Then no one will be able to control you.

One who is learning should be passionate and serious. One must build upon the skills one has learned in practice. One must acquire continuous courage to master *dori* (the way of things).

There is an equation to victory.

One can become a master through experience and by practicing and learning tactics.

Combine your power and your opponent's power to use your technique without letting your opponent know. One should use technique without revealing it to the adversary. By the time the adversary recognizes the technique, one must have brought the adversary down.

Fudoshin (Immovable Mind)

1. Overcoming life and death, not fearing death and escaping death are different things.
2. One can establish the state of *fudoshin* through training but this is different than protecting one's body.
3. Training to protect one's body and mind are two different things.
4. In martial arts, one will be equipped with the power to protect *fudoshin* and life by training the mind, techniques, and body to be consistent.

Perfecting *Michi* (the Path)

In order to perfect *michi*, one should not be misled by bad phenomena which meet one's eye.

Do not be distracted by surrounding noise.
Do not become conceited by flattering speech and conduct.
Keep a tight rein over oneself and be generous to others.

Allow one to enjoy *cyudo* (moderation) in life. Everything in life has *michi*. Being conscious that life is a *dojo* (a training hall) will open the path to *budo* (the martial arts).

BURYAK AND *BUDO* (STRATEGY AND THE MARTIAL ARTS)

The martial arts entail strategy.
Strategy is *hei-ho* (the art of war).
Hei-ho depends on how one can trick his or her adversary.

In a fight, one must not forget deception.
Deception makes an object more possible than shedding someone's blood.
One must become like a panther during hunting.
A panther takes a very long path around to hunt.
On occasion as a strategy, a panther lets the quarry get away.

In *Hei-ho*, there is a stratagem in which one collects all the information of an adversary to confuse and isolate him or her.

An ideology of *hei-ho* today requires arming oneself.

In order to grow, one must have a rival.
A rival could be oneself or one's adversary.

Mindless (*Mushin*) Victory

One must reach a state of mindlessness in order to have a mindless victory.
At the state of mindlessness, one does not have ulterior motives and one's *honshin* (original mind) is attentive and accurate.
Mushin is one's presence of mind.

One's presence of mind, then, is courage.
Without courage, techniques cannot be utilized to the fullest.
The only way to cultivate courage is through hard training at a *dojo* (training hall).
Training is the only way to gain courage and not to be easily frightened.

Through training, one reaches the state of mindlessness. Only then, will one be able to discard the thoughts of anxiety, the opponent's technique and defenses. Being in the state of mindlessness means to entrust one's mind and body to the universe.

One can reach *mushin* by letting go of one's obsession and collect truth in the mind. Then, one can see the adversary's intention clearly.
Not missing a chance to strike is mindless victory.

Kyo and *Jitsu* (Void and One's Actual Ability)

Kyo (void) is *jitsu* (one's actual ability) to make a tricky move.
Jitsu is *sei* (truth).

Ki (falsity) and *sei* transform into each other.
Kyo (void) is *jitsu*. *Jitsu* is *kyo*.

The Four Conditions to Victory

1. Understand the advantages and disadvantages of the adversary.
2. Take the initiative and observe the adversary's moves.
3. Let the adversary throw his or her strategic moves to find the keys.
4. Set a reconnoitering skirmish. Find the strengths and weaknesses in the adversary's style.

Kisei (Falsity and Truth Transform Each Other) Corresponds to an Adversary's *Kyo* and *Jitsu*

1. When an adversary is in *jitsu*
   —If one's fighting strength is at its peak, make a fair attack.
2. When an adversary is in *kyo*
   —If one's fighting strength is weak, respond with *ki* (void).
3. You should make changes in *kisei*
   —Position of *kiyojitsu* will become the adversary's issue.
4. Victory and defeat depends on taking the initiative and how one fights.
5. Flexibility to change one's stance from *ki* to *sei* will give you an advantage and keep the adversary occupied.
   —Falsity can be truth. Truth can be falsity.

HOW TO GRASP POWER

One should always have a calm, cautious, and disciplined attitude towards an adversary. The following points must be noted:

1. Make a first move and wait for the opponent's thrust.
2. Wait for the opponent to create blindness.
3. Wait for the opponent to move around.
4. Wait for the opponent to lose control.
5. Wait for the opponent to be confused.
6. Wait for the opponent to attack with a solid defense.

By following and keeping the above in mind, one can grasp the power to achieve victory.

CHAPTER 2

The Meaning of *Tanren*

The meaning of *tanren* (discipline, training) lies in the effort to burn out the energy of one's mind and body with burning flames. *Tanren* requires mental integration and concentration that lead to the deep root.

One can acquire resistance by going through *tanren*. Once one acquires resistance, one is able to withstand pain. Once one acquires a durable mind, exquisite sense will be fostered. Once exquisite sense is sharpened, one's external consciousness and subconscious connect. When they connect, one acquires spiritual power. Once one acquires spiritual power, one will be able to cope with things naturally.

Tanren

FEAR

Fear is something one has to get over through *tanren*. To get over it, one needs to train one's observation on the mind and develop the strength of will.

When one becomes conscious by sensing the function of mind and the truth of the universe, one's fear disappears.

Kugyou (Penance)

Tanren (training) must not be *kugyou* (punishment). Do not forget that *higi* (secret tactics) exists in enjoyment.

How to acquire *higi*:

1. Have an open mind. Stay calm and composed.
2. Always be considerate of yourself and others.
3. Lend your ear to many people.
4. Become aware of your real feelings and discard your obsessions.
5. Feel regret for what you have done. Although feeling regret cannot take back what you have done, it can change your opponent and yourself.
6. Always have joy in your mind.

OBSTRUCTIONS TO TRAINING

Dou

Dou never answers in words. It makes you realize the existence of internal wisdom of the mind. It shows you the way of life. It teaches that the way you are is the truth.

People are swayed by worldly desire and obsessions. You don't have to worry. While you have a life, do the best you can. When you die, you simply need to die.

Satori is achieved when your mind and the mind of the universe connect. When they connect, you start to bear supernatural power.

The World of *Ku*

While you are in meditation, there is a moment when you don't hear any sound. There is a moment when only reverberations remain. When you are in the quiet moment, you are standing at the gateway to *ku*, where the power of mighty nature exists. You are standing at the gateway to *sinmyo-uryoku* (superhuman power) that is considered to be *mu*, the ultimate in technique. And in the world of *sinmyouryoku*, you see quick movements in slow motion. At that moment, you reach the gateway where geniuses and saints have reached.

Do not mistake the gate for the house (the truth) that stands inside.

Do not forget that you are on a parallel with the training to enable the low-layer fourth-dimensional *sii*, which draws negative power.

The most important thing is to use the mind of *chudou* as a monitor and carry out your goal of attaining *satori* of higher levels.

The internal fight is to try to control your fate by learning to control your spirit and feelings during a fight and facing the result of your decision and choice.

KNOWLEDGE OF TRAINING

1. Consider the mind to be pure, innocent, and good-natured. You should not violate it.
2. Be aware of a feeling for others.
3. Believe that by brushing up and enriching your mind you become a distinguished person.
4. You can only do things within the size of your caliber. Be aware of the training of creating your caliber. When your mind is rich, you have the caliber than can sense spiritual power.
5. Believe that spiritual power and mental power exist in the invisible world, soundless world, and insensible world.
6. Be aware of the fact that the mighty nature and the great universe are your textbooks.
7. Discover that the mind is greater than the universe.
8. Conquer your fear.
9. Appreciate the joy of having a life in this world.

Obstructions to Training

Obstructions to training are desire for money, an appetite for power, sexual appetite, a hunger for fame, desire for scents, desire for voice, desire for tastes, sensual appetite, a hunger for law, joy, anger, enjoyment, fear, jealousy, lust, and so on.

Anything should not be beyond *chudou* (middle of balance, center). If the mind is obsessed, it bears worldly desire and creates a cause of *ku* (trouble).

MU AND *KYUDOU* (JAPANESE ARCHERY)

Kenzou Kawami, known as *kyusei* (master of Japanese archery) had the following philosophy of *mu* for *kyudou*.

To hit the target, it has to be as if the arrow heads toward the target voluntarily, regardless of your aim. You need to be *mu* to achieve it. When you are *mu*, the arrow you shoot will naturally hit the target without your aiming at it. It is not to hit but to be hit.

Keep looking at the target until it starts to blur, and then close your eyes. When you close your eyes, you feel as if the target is approaching toward you. The target and you become one. God and you become one. When these are united, they become immovable center. Then, the arrow hits the center of the target. The arrow goes out from a center and goes into a center. The arrow hits the target. When you reach this state, do not aim at the target, aim at yourself. Hit both the targets of you and God at one time.

Kenzou described the secret of *kyudou* as follows. When you come to know who to see, what to see, and who to put in instead of you, you don't need a mentor any longer.

A Record of a Dialogue Between Musashi and Lord Hosokawa

Musashi stands for Musashi Miyamoto (1584–1645). He left a great name behind him as author of *Goryinsyo*, which is now read as a utilitarian and practical book.

Lord Hosakawa stands for Lord Tadaaki Hosokawa (1588–1642). He was the lord of the area that is now called Kumamoto City. Musashi served him.

Lord Hosakawa :	You say that you risked your life more than 100 times in deadly duels. Were there any opponents who seemed formidable?
Musashi :	They were all great sword fighters.
Lord Hosakawa :	While you were in a duel, haven't you ever been afraid that you might lose?
Musashi :	Never.
Lord Hosakawa :	Life is very dear to every human being. I suppose every swordsman must think about life when he meets the opponent who is more skillful than him. How about you?
Musashi :	I have never learned swordplay from a master. I train

	myself in the mountains. I hang dozens of strings from branches of trees and strike them at random from below, the strings rebound. My swordplay is the extremity of the timing of not being hit by the strings. You cannot win humans' duels if you see the duel as killing each other. I dodge the branches so that they do not hit me. I only deal with the opponents in the same way.
Lord Hosakawa :	Why do you do that?
Musashi :	Trees do not fear. Only I feel the fear. When I fight against human beings, my opponent fears me and he escapes from my sword. The strings hanging from the trees never escape. When I fight against the strings, I sometimes lose and get hit. However, I never have been defeated nor hit in humans' duels.

When your mind is positive, it is not weak. When your mind is absolute, you don't feel that you are fighting to dear life even during a deadly duel.

There are two kinds of positive. As for the secrets of swordplay, if you become defensive to the opponent's technique, your body becomes defensive and then you lose your balance. You should not be defensive, just fend off the attack.

Similarly, as for events in your life, you should disregard them as if they were swords that attack you at random. Then, the opponent will stumble on oneself and falter.

—From a Record of a Dialogue between Musashi and Lord Hosakawa.

Fudoshin

CHAPTER 3

Tactics for Actual Fighting

Waza – Techniques

The martial arts training starts from sensitizing five senses.

In the beginning, learn how arms and legs function, then learn how to use *waza*. You will then continue to train your concentration and unification of mind, learn to sharpen your cautiousness, association, and inspiration. After you learn those basics, intensify you inner life energy and train to achieve super power.

To intensify your life energy, it is necessary to practice *waza* repeatedly. When you drive yourself to the edge of death physically and mentally, your sensitivity will be sharpened and your life energy will be intensified.

By intensifying your life energy, you will be close to the state of emptiness. Once you reach the state of emptiness, you can manage your *waza* without consciously trying. The first-class unbeatable arts will then be completed.

All the training is done to achieve the movements of unconsciousness. Training is meant to forget training after repetitions. If you are conscious of your *waza*, it is not real yet.

THE STATE OF *FUDO* AND *FUDO-SHIN*

Fudo – Stable, nonmovable.
Fudo-shin – Stable mind

Some of the most important things in fighting are the state of *fudo* and *fudo-shin*.

The state of *fudo*

The state of *fudo* is a condition that cannot be moved or changed by anything.

Techniques, sensitivity, experiences, and many other factors count to be a skilled athlete.

When you confront someone with abilities, you cannot set off your *waza* as you wish. Those strong ones can read what you will do next.

The non-beatable *fudo* state can be attained by training *fudo-shin*.

Fudo-shin

Mind and body are deeply connected to each other with full concentration.

Fudo-shin means that you let go of clinging and firmly believe that you won't be beaten by anything.

THINGS TO KEEP IN MIND WHILE FIGHTING

Eye levels and eye light (*ganko*)

Eyes are an important factor for pre-fighting. Eye level and eye lights will be the greatest factor to determine the outcome.

If you look with a light in your eyes, your mind could be out of focus and affect your movement.

If you look with power in your eyes, your mental power lowers as well; you can get caught off guard.

Eyes are the energy resources of your body, mind and *waza*. It is ideal that your eyes hold power, lights, freshness, and liveliness.

Posture

When you round your back, energy will become trapped inside your body and become negative energy. When you straighten your back, energy will flow more smoothly. Energy will start to go out and become positive.

Straightening your posture makes your breathing smooth.

Opening up your chest and straightening your body will open up your heart.

Opening up your heart and breathing into your core will eliminate your stress.

An assertive posture can be attained by learning how to manage your body.

Kiai—snarling, releasing inner energy out loud

Kiai is a shouting out of words within you and expressing your feelings.
When you *kiai*, you should lean forward mentally and physically.
Kiai should be short and sharp so it penetrates the other's heart.

The sound also works as lowering the blood pressure of the person who listens to it and it can partially deaden the other's senses. Good *kiai* can blow out your thoughts and doubts. It can beat up your opponent with willpower. The low frequency of sound—3.5 cycles per second—can also kill a person.

Before you *kiai*, you should capture the opponent's figure, like a lion aiming its prey, and be prepared to take everything from him.

It is best if a *kiai* can take out the opponent's energy with your opponent. *Kiai* can work like hypnotism.

Kiai has a magical power to diminish and purify the bad ghosts. You should learn how to pull this power out of your body.

Footwork

Use footwork to disrupt your opponent's timing and focus. Footwork consists of offense and defense. It is necessary to gain momentum by movement.

If you wish to wait for the chance to counter attack against an opponent who is stronger than you, you should keep moving around the opponent until you confuse him.

Start attacking once you see a change. As soon as your first attack, take back where you can't be reached. Your footwork should be continuous and fast.

If you want to wait for the other to attack you, take rhythms with your footwork and try to counter. Concentrate.

Favorite Technique

Everyone has his favorite way of attack; one who likes to trick, one who attacks first, one who waits for the turn, one who likes to jump, one who likes to throw, one who likes to let go. People all have favorite ways of attacking.

Sense the other's favorite. Let him attack in the way he likes. If you know his favorite, you can counter him.

The Way to See How Skillful Your Opponent is

Anyone who deals with *waza* needs to be bold. Once you get the opportunity, pat your opponent's arms or legs. If she/he can softly ward you off, you can assume she/he could be a good competitor.

Small *Waza*, Big *Waza*

When you deal with *waza*, you should straighten your back, elbows and knees.

One who has a small body tends to rely on small *waza*, and one who has a big body tends to rely on big *waza*. Therefore, one who has a small body should try to develop big *waza*; one who has a big body should try to develop small *waza*. Keep a good balance of your *waza*.

THE BASIC KNOWLEDGE OF ARMS

Mental Practice

There are two kinds of practice—physical practice and mental practice. During practice, if your arms tighten up, your *waza* will be small. If your back gets round, your arms tighten up.

If you can keep a straight posture, your arms can be relaxed and free. Your arms can be straight and your *waza* can travel fast. *Waza* can be more alive by straightening your posture.

Footwork

Taking too big a step or too small a step, you can be easily knocked down by sweeping.

Choose footwork that can go well with your *waza*. Your footwork should be stable so your weight stays down. Your powerhouse interacts well with good footwork.

Three Basics about *waza*

There are three ways to set off your *waza*.

1. *Kuzushi* (Breaking Down)—Break down the opponent's posture and make room for your attack.
2. *Tsukuri* (Building Up)—Plunge your opponent further into an unstable situation.

3. *Kake* (Setting)—set your *waza* to your opponent.
    Take your opponent off guard by breaking him down. Take the lead in the fight. Finally, set your *waza* and beat him.

When you set *waza* use your willpower and momentum while you stay relaxed mentally. Try the opposite of what the opponent thinks. Always aim opposite. By taking the lead, you can force the opponent to your pace. Beginners, take the first turn and attack positively.

The Basics of Heart and Mental Power
1. *Kokoro* (heart)—From the quiet moment, aim the opponent off guard. Concentrate and do not miss unguarded moments.
2. *Ki* (Inner Energy)—The momentum of inner energy.
3. *Chikara* (Power)—Power and the strength of your *waza*.

Four Rules about *Waza*
1. Do not be alarmed or afraid of your opponent's *waza*. When you are afraid of your opponent's *waza*, you can't attack normally. If you are lost, you will be unguarded.
2. Do not be unsure. When you are unsure, you will be reckless. Recklessness will slow your body movement. It further allows your opponent to sense your hastiness and gives him a chance to attack first.
3. Do not doubt your *waza*. Whatever your *waza* is, go with a positive mind. Be very forward.
4. Do not back off. Backing off mentally and being defensive will give your opponent a chance to attack. You will also lose your chance to attack back. Pep yourself up with *kiai* and heighten your energy.

Positive Defense
The most sophisticated defense prevents the opponent's offense beforehand and doesn't let him touch you. It is a very positive way of handling the fight. You are always ready to attack back.

There is the saying "offense is the greatest defense." The real defense comes from identification of offense and defense.

The Objective of Training with a Partner (*Kumite*)

The object of *kumite* is to train you to find the opponent's unguarded moments. A calm state of mind is necessary. You can find your way to survive when you reach the point beyond life.

Let go of the opponent's impact like water. Once you shift to offense from defense, your offence must have great momentum like a storm. In order to accomplish ideal *kumite*, you need to know the breathing of offense and defense, the truth of negative and positive. That will lead you to the unconditional *kumite*.

When you train by yourself, think of yourself confronted by multiple opponents. When you train with others, think of a situation where you confront all of them by yourself.

Things to Keep in Mind When You Train with Others (*Kumite*)

When you confront others, keep your mind open. Present yourself profoundly as if you can engulf the other. Prepare yourself so you can throw your *waza* in a moment. That is the basic of *kamae* (preparing). To prepare yourself mentally, remember the truth of *fudo-shin*.

Managing Your Body

There is a saying about *kumite*. Receive internally then externally. Control yourself then absorb attacks internally. Techniques of managing your body should be safe and effective.

Things to Keep in Mind When You Practice

1. Always practice with passion. When you lack concentration and passion, you invite injuries.
2. When you learn *waza*, try to learn everything to keep the balance.
3. Developing your mental state is more important than learning skills.

Basics of Breathing When You Practice

1. During practice, close your mouth and breathe through your nose.
2. When you collect your breathing, inhale through your nose and exhale with your mouth using your *tanden* (powerhouse).
3. After intensive training, you must not stop suddenly. Keep moving your body mildly until your breathing settles down.

Tricking your Opponent

Tricking your opponent makes him want to guess your next movement. Deceive him and put him into an off-balanced situation.

Once the first movement is ordered in the brain, the brain can't go to the next movement until the first action is stopped. If that delay is 50 millimeters per second, a basketball would travel 35 centimeters.

Training *Waza* Depending on your Height

1. Short people are good at in-close fighting. Train *waza* for in-close fighting. Build up your offense and defense skills.
2. Tall people can attack from farther away. Train *waza* that can reach far. Build up your defense skill.
3. Powerful people should learn *waza* that has forward power. Strengthen your defense.

Everyone should learn waza that covers their weaknesses.

How to Take the Initial Turn of Attacking

Take the initial turn of attack before the opponent composes himself for the fight.

1. Attack before his preparation position is ready.
2. Attack before he is mentally ready.

Iki-oi

The Basics of the Ready Position (*Kamae*)

You always want to break down your opponent's *kamae*. You always want to keep a *kamae* that is difficult to attack.

Kamae should be focused on the center of the body. It is said that the ultimate ready position is in the center.

The *waza* of karate needs momentum. It is not good to have tension in your shoulders. Keep your back straight, keep circulating your energy, keep the position so *waza* can reach well and you can increase the speed of reaching. The ready position should be strong for offense and defense.

Ready position can be categorized into four groups:

The Natural Preparation

In order to complete the natural preparation, keep your mind free of thought while you sustain an intense drive within you. When your body is in offensive mode, your mind is in defensive mode. Keep your mind in offensive mode while your body is in defensive mode.

The Ready Position of Circle Form (*Enso*)

Grip your hand lightly as if your hands are blooming flowers. Keep your arms' end lower than the shoulder. When you reach your hands out, your elbow should be rounded as if you are drawing a circle. The idea is that you almost extend over your arms. Your heart should enfold the opponents. Put your energy into your powerhouse.

The Ready Position of Inducement (*Yu-in*)

The ready position of inducement is a preparation form to induce the opponent to attack. There are upper *kamae* and lower *kamae*. For upper *kamae*, open your middle and lower body and invite the other's attack there. For lower *kamae*, leave your face unguarded and wait for the other to attack your face. Invite the expected attack and attack him back.

The Preparation of Emptiness or No-Self (*Muga*)

The preparation of emptiness leads the opponent to throw his strongest *waza* so you can aim him afterwards.

* Reveal everything to your opponent and sustain the state of emptiness.

There should be no doubt. The opponent can detect your doubt and you will lose your rhythm.

* By revealing everything, you will make him believe that he can win. He will then attack with his strongest *waza*. You can ward off the *waza* and take control over him.
* This can be effective with the opponent whom you can't beat normally. Put him off guard by making him believe it is an easy match. You can then lead the match and win.
* The preparation of emptiness is effective when you are about to die.

The Basics of Distance between You and the Opponent (*Maai*)

Maai is a space between you and the opponent where you each seek the next move. Keep *maai* changing in the opponent's eyes. It is necessary to control *maai* with an empty mind. One who can control the space of *maai* can manage good conditions to win. Carrying out conditioned stamina, skills, and mental training is necessary.

How to take control of the ideal space between you and the opponent (maai).

With novice opponents, step in and practice your defensive skills. With opponents of your level, take one step in and be ready to get into the opponent's territory. With unknown opponents, choose to fight from a greater distance. Keep the distance so you can observe the opponent's movement. Once you see a chance, immediately attack.

CHAPTER 4

How to Take Maximum Advantage of your *Waza*

If you think too much before you set off your *waza*, it doesn't reach well; it gives your opponent a chance to attack back.

When you set off your *waza*, avoid confronting your opponent from the front as much as you can. Change the angle and attack.

When you attack, you shouldn't expect to beat the opponent with only one *waza*. When you concentrate too much on a single *waza*, your energy will shrink and the next continuous *waza* will not come along.

When the opponent wards off your blow and starts counter-attacking, overwhelm him with your energy.

Waza

STRONG *WAZA*, WEAK *WAZA*

In karate, there are different kinds of *waza*; jabbing (*tsuki*), kicking (*keri*), receiving (*uke*), parrying (*nagasu*), throwing (*nogeru*), holding (*osae*), tightening (*shimeru*), and joints (*kansetsu*).

You do not need to know all kinds of *waza*, but it is good to know several kinds of *waza* in each category. By knowing different *waza*, you can guess what kind of *waza* the opponent is using. You can then counter the opponent's attack successfully.

When you attack, try using a *waza* that the opponent is not good at receiving. To the opponent who is good at kicking but not good at arm techniques, use arm techniques. Target his weak point.

Actual Fighting and Practice

You cannot differentiate between the practice and the actual fight. You will lose energy and concentration if you do.

Practice *waza* correctly. When you practice, always think of the actual fight. Prepare mentally and condition yourself physically.

How to Manage Opponents with Weapons.
1. Do not look at the weapon.
2. Do not be afraid of death. Keep your mind calm. Move fast. Catch your opponent off guard.
3. Impede your opponent's sight by throwing sand or objects into his eyes and get a change.
4. Know how to use weapons in different situations.

How to Use Restraint (*Kensei*)

Restrain your opponent's energy so he can't use it. Aim at his throat. When you restrain someone, you can't only think about your defense, or you would be doubtful and give the opponent a chance to attack.

When the opponent is controlling you, keep your energy high. Do not let him control you. Ward him off. Overwhelm him with your energy so you don't get overwhelmed yourself. Do not let your opponent control you the way he wants. Outsmart him. You need to have a momentum of mental and physical energy.

The perfect restraint can restrict the opponent's will, energy and intentions.

Attacking Each Other at the Same Time

If the opponent attacks your upper body, you should attack his middle area at the same time. When attacking happens at the same time, attack contrasting or different parts of the body.

If the opponent moves, that means he has stepped into your space (*maai*). From the ready position, attack without hesitation. Control your opponent's movement first. Attack him with the momentum of mindset, energy flow, and power. Attack with continuous *waza* and give him no chance to attack back.

How to Take the First Turn

When you sense that your opponent is about to attack you, move first so you can restrain his start. Beginners should take the first turn to win. Once you approach your opponent, take the initiative to attack with momentum and rhythm. Keep your *waza* coming fast.

Fill yourself with a flow of energy (*ki*). Set off your *waza* with momentum and overwhelm the opponent. There is only a single chance to beat him. Any initiative *waza* should come from you decisively. Use all your energy when you move offensively and defensively. When not moving offensively or defensively, conserve your energy.

When your opponent is getting ready to release his *waza*, he will concentrate on his *waza*. He will lose concentration on other places. You can find an opening to attack. Aim at the moment before or after the opponent's *waza* is set off. Let him miss a shot and get that moment when his balance is off. Sense the waza that the opponent's starting off and take the initiative turn.

When you are starting off the initiative *waza*, do not be nervous. Be bold and have a brave heart. Without an initiative move, there is no winning.

How to Make Use of Your Strong *Waza*

Study what you are good at and build up so you can have *waza* that can beat anyone. Study the positioning, spacing, and stepping in and out of the spaces. Learn counter-techniques (*kaeshi-waza*) correctly. Do not break your positioning after you attack.

Even if your first *waza* doesn't work, continue with more techniques. Be calm and composed so you can cover your weaknesses.

Strengthen your favorite technique and make it perfect. Make it something you can be confident with.

When Your Opponent's Energy and Your Energy Hit Each Other at the Same Time

When your opponent comes to attack you with full energy, calm your energy first and then build up your energy in a second. Overwhelm him. When you see him hesitate, attack him all the way.

On the other hand, when your opponent comes to attack you with calm energy, keep your posture higher and straighten your back. Step in to him fast and attack him sharply as if you are stepping on his energy.

How to Deal With Body Attacking Techniques (*Atemi-Waza*)
Body attacking needs momentum and speed. When the opponent's energy is full, body attacking doesn't work.

Chnces to attack the body should be taken at the end of exhaling, the end of speaking, the end of movement, the moment the opponent's power lowers or the moment the opponent's shoulders go down.

How to Dominate the Opponent
Knowing your opponent well and catching him in off guard moments will be the basis of fights. Sustaining energy is necessary in fights. Do not lose your flow of energy. When the situation looks bad for you, see the situation well and judge. Judge the ability, advantages, and disadvantages.

If there is no flow of energy, there is no winning.

The Way to Make Use of Surprise
When two people are confronting each other and there is no off-guard moment, clap your hands in front of your opponent and surprise him. When you clap your hands and your opponent gets surprised, that is the moment to attack.

OFFENSE AND DEFENSE
Taking offense means offending the opponent's mentality. It is also about knowing the opponent. Taking defense means fulfilling your flow of energy and waiting for the situation to change.

Fulfilling your inner energy helps you to know about yourself.

Whether you can see a chance of winning depends on the opponent's situation. When you attack the opponent's mental state, try psychological attacks and take his intentions away. When you heighten your energy, fill your inner energy and wait for the chance to attack. Attacking mentality means taking the energy off the opponent. When you can do that, you can be a great athlete, a great director.

Know your opponent and know yourself.

HOW TO SEE THE CHANCE TO START OFF YOUR *WAZA*
The Chance to Start Off Your *Waza*
* When the opponent is starting their *waza*.
* The moment you ward off the opponent's *waza*.
* The moment the opponent takes back to ward off the attack.
* The moment the opponent's energy spreads.

The Strong *Waza*, the Weak *Waza*
Anyone has his weak point in techniques. Aim at the weak points. Build up stable defense in your weak points. Fulfill energy to make use of your *waza*.

Avoid the Situations You Can't Handle
Waza should be used with combinations. In a bad situation, go back to the original position so the opponent can't reach you. Avoid bad situations and wait for the next chance.

Setting Off *Waza* that Contrasts the Opponent's *Waza*.
When the opponent attacks your upper body, attack back to the middle. When the opponent attacks you with legs, attack him back with arms.

Set off the waza that contradicts each other.

How to Take a Chance by Inviting Attack
When you set your ready position in the upper position, you will have a space in the middle part. Make space intentionally and invite the opponent to attack there. Wait for the moment he attacks.

When you fake an attack, the opponent's energy will be tense. Aim at the point after the tensed energy gets loosened up.

Make yourself look like you are weak. When the opponent starts to attack, make it look like you are running away. Once the opponent loosens up, take the chance and attack.

Patiently Wait for a Chance and Set Off *Waza*

When you patiently wait for a chance to set off your *waza*, both the opponent's *waza* and your *waza* could hit off each other and negate each other. In such a case, overwhelm the opponent with heightened energy. That will make your *waza* strong.

In the situation where your *waza* doesn't work when you try to set it off, do something completely different and bold. Attack a part that your opponent wouldn't even expect and confuse his judgment. You will then find a way.

How to Set Your Opponent Off-Guard

Make yourself look like you are setting off hand techniques, but set off leg techniques instead.

Make yourself look like you are moving all of a sudden. Your opponent will attack physically. Aim at that moment.

Always set your mind to believe that you will never lose, never take back.

When the Opponent Holds and You Can't Use Your *Waza*

Push him with your shoulders.

Use throwing *waza*.

How to Chase Opponents

Chase your opponent to the poorly situated ground and stand on the better ground. When you chase, chase the opponent to the left and keep a big space on your left.

Hitting the Opponent Hard

When blocking, hit the opponent hard, as if you are breaking his arms and legs.

Receiving and attacking should be done at the same time so the opponent doesn't have a chance to set off his *waza*.

When you hit your opponent hard, beat him until you take his energy completely out so he can never set off his second *waza*. Do not let him stand up. Kill his chance of attacking back.

When You Attack His Mental

Look through your mind's eye rather than your physical eyes. Do not look at the opponent's arms and legs. Look at his heart (mind).

Do not set your eyes on his eyes because he will sense it.

Never repeat the *waza* that was a mistake.

When Your Lower Body is High

During the fight, your body tends to lose its lower position. This will make you feel fidgety. Keep low in your ready position—it makes offense and defense easier.

The ultimate *waza* doesn't need so much technique. Most of the time it only needs one shot. Lower your body and fulfill your energy.

Waza by Masters

A master of *waza* is liberated. He would never miss a moment. It looks easy and calm. *Waza* shouldn't be set off in a rush.

1. Put yourself in the opponent's shoes. You will then get rid of your worries.
2. You can achieve chances by training. Thousands of punches and kicks are called training. Thousands of training sessions are called discipline. *Waza* can only be achieved by repeating. There is no other way. That is how human bodies are made.

Aiki

TAKE ADVANTAGE OF ENERGY MEETING (*AIKI*)

When your energy and the opponent's energy meet, it is called *aiki* or *waki*. *Aiki* will make changes in *waza*. When your *waza* takes your opponent's energy, your *waza* works as you wish. That is because your energy overwhelms the other and his energy dies.

When you look with composition in your heart, you will lose the balance in your movement. Your physical movement gets tense.

When your energy wanders around, you cannot set off your *waza* as you wish.

Work your energy correctly. That will give you a change in *waza* to take initiative in the fight.

Fights are about competition of energy and competition of *waza*.

How to Ward off the Energy Meeting (*Aiki*)

Energy meeting is a *waza* that removes the opponent's freedom. Once you complete extraordinary concentration, you can obtain *waza* that takes the power of the opponent's in the moment your waza meets each other.

In the situations that the opponent has strong energy, you should receive it with weak energy.

When the opponent has weak energy, you should receive it with strong energy.

It is called breaking off the matching energy when you set off the energy that goes against the opponent's and makes him irresistible.

How to Chase the Energy

You want to chase your opponent when your energy is fulfilled more and your situation is better.

When the opponent's position is stable, do not set off *waza* against the situation. Wait for a chance.

When you chase the opponent, if the opponent manages *waza* and keeps changing his offense, chase him as you change angles and combine your *waza*.

You can't follow the opponent who wants to run away for too long or you will lose your energy. You have to be careful.

How to Counter Off Flow of Energy (*Ki*)

There is a kind of *waza* to ward off the technique from an opponent while taking advantage of his *waza*.

1. When the opponent is attacking, let go of the other's energy as you back off. Take that moment.
2. Take the moment when the opponent finishes with his first *waza* and goes to the next one.
3. Raise your energy higher than the opponent's when he attacks you. Break his rhythm and keep attacking.
4. If you cling to his energy, you will also lose a chance.
5. When you deal with your own body, do it fully. Do not let the opponent's *waza* touch you.

How to Use Energy Invitation

There is an invitation (*yu-in*) way to take an initiative in a fight.

1. *Waza* of invitation cannot be accomplished when there is fear in your energy.
2. When the opponent's energy and your energy become equal, they hit off each other. It will be the battle of *waza* and *ki*.
3. When the opponent's position is broken down by invitation, invitation becomes successful. When you make yourself look like your energy is weakening, the opponent can be invited to lower his energy.
4. Take the chance when the opponent is affected by the invitation and start off his *waza*.

5. When the opponent sets off *waza* as if he bought your invitation, set off your *waza* and get what he is aiming at in one step forward.

    Invitation that has full mental and physical knowledge can control the other.

When the Opponent's Energy is in Offensive Mode

When the opponent's energy is higher than yours, set firm defense, then sense your opponent's next move. If you can sense it, set off your *waza* in advance.

Ward off the opponent's *waza* right and left, shifting your body. Wait for a chance his *waza* is finished.

When you Fight Multiple Opponents

Take advantage of the landscape. Narrow space works well when you confront many opponents. Wait in the narrow space. Confront them in badly situated land like mountains. Set so the opponent has to attack you one by one. Use strategy.

BOOK TWO

BASIC LAWS OF THE
MIND AND BODY

CHAPTER 1

Basic Laws of the Mind and Body

The structure and movement of the body are governed by the basic laws of nature. The structure of the human body is such that when one part of the body moves, other parts of the body will move accordingly as a result. Exercising without the knowledge of these laws of nature can result in misalignment of the skeletal structure, which may lead to emotional or physical disorders.

Shu Chu Ryoku

BASIC RULES OF FIGHTING

Kiai

Kiai (mental vigor) is important in combat as well as in business situations. At a critical moment, do not retreat even in the face of death.

About the Body

When your body is slouched forward, the airflow in the chest may be obstructed, causing a deficiency in oxygen. Insufficient oxygen can weaken your hips, resulting in poor concentration.

Try to keep your spine straight, with the hips slightly lowered. Relax your shoulders to sharpen up your mind and skill. The hips play a pivotal role in keeping the mind and body sharp.

When the hips are weak, your ability to concentrate diminishes. Weak-mindedness and indecisiveness occur when your attention is diverted from your hips.

Do not overstretch your hips when executing karate techniques.

Being alert in mind and body can help you better deal with a challenging task.

Any shift in body movement originates from the hips. You need to become conscious of the movement of your hips. Loosen up your limbs and relax your joints.

Positive and Negative Forces

Nature is dominated by *yin* and *yang*. There are positive and negative forces, and good and evil on this planet. Great achievements are always followed by failures of the similar magnitude. Do not let your guard down in times of happiness. Life requires mental strength that enables one to cope calmly with unfortunately events. Always be prepared for something bad to happen.

When you feel that your body is filled with negative energy, try to reverse it by listening to, reading, or observing something positive. In order to do that, you will need a yardstick by which to evaluate your progress.

When something is gained, something will be lost. You pay a certain price for happiness. Everyone will have to pay for their mistakes. Positive and negative forces offset each other. Be aware of the fact that life always entails death.

Right Attitudes toward Learning

Before you attempt to learn something new, deepen your existing knowledge, broaden your mind, and improve your character. By doing so, your soul will shine everlastingly even when you are dressed in tatters.

How to Acquire Knowledge

If your knowledge is limited to relevant information, your brain will overheat and slow down. To cool down your overheated brain, you also need to feed your brain with miscellaneous information. In other words, your knowledge should be well rounded.

Good Strategy

Those who develop extraordinary ability spare no effort to enhance their own value.

1. Third-rate Strategy—Uses one's own ability
2. Second-rate Strategy—Uses other people's ability.
3. First-rate Strategy—Uses other people's wisdom.
4. A Leader's Strategy—Makes full use of one's subordinates ability.
5. A Saint's Strategy—Accomplishes a great feat in a state of self-effacement.

BASIC EXERCISE

Our health is influenced by factors such as breathing, food and drink, mental and physical condition, behavior, and environment.

Proper breathing is the key to staying healthy. Martial artists practice *chosoku*, which is a method for controlling breathing patters. Through respiration, oxygen in the air is taken into the lungs, where it enters the bloodstream. Red blood cells that carry oxygen significantly affect the balance of vital energy within the body. Chosoku places special emphasis on exhalation.

Correct breathing, a proper diet, adequate physical exercise, logical thinking, and right action (consciously or unconsciously) are very important in our lives. When any one of these components is neglected, the balance of your body will be disturbed. Proper body balance varies for each person, depending on his ability.

Tanden is situated below the navel. Pay special attention to *tanden* during exhalation. You need to focus your mind on breathing so that your breathing pattern is in harmony with the workings of your mind. *Chushin-ten* can be located by focusing your eyes, mind, and body on a single point.

When your body is out of alignment, it will not function normally even with a good diet and proper breathing. Moreover, misalignment of the body structure can give rise to symptoms such as stiffness in the shoulders.

Greediness can upset the balance of the mind and body. Unnatural movements not only disturb *chushin-ten* (central point) in the body but can also contribute to injuries or ailments.

Nothing is a tragic as being unable to appreciate what you have. You will have peace of mind by being appreciative of your life, the natural world, and the blessings of nature.

Our lives are sustained by the blessings of nature and other people's affection. You must show genuine affection toward others and give verbal support to raise their spirits.

What lies at the heart of our action is kindness.

CHUSHIN-TEN OF POWER

Chushin-ten (central point) of the body is situated in the hips. An athlete can boost his physical efficiency by using the hips as the foundation of all movements. During exercise, the hips should be kept slightly low. Focusing your energy on *chushin-ten* of the body can enhance your physical strength, minimize fatigue and add beauty to your motions.

When *chushin-ten* of the body is misaligned, it can impede the normal functions of the mind. The mind and body are two sides of the same coin. The feeling of sadness causes your body to slouch and your head to droop. When in high spirits, your hips naturally straighten up. Fatigue occurs when *chushin-ten* of the body goes out of alignment, disturbing the balance of the motor system.

Enhance your physical strength by consciously contracting the muscles of the little fingers while keeping your elbows at the sides of your body. The farther way the elbows are from your body, the less energy you will have.

While engaged in a task that requires manual dexterity, raising your shoulders and keeping your thumbs inside can damage your shoulders. Shoulder-ache is caused by unnatural stiffening of your muscles.

A projected chin is a sign of fatigue. That is when *chushin-ten* of your body goes out of alignment. When the mind is twisted, the body will become crooked. When your mind is at peace, the muscles of the lower abdomen naturally contract. Anger makes the upper abdomen tense, which can lead to liver dysfunction. Emotion and respiration are interrelated. When in a difficult situation, try to smile to relieve your tension.

Chushin-ten of the body is situated in *tanden*, which is located on the third lumbar vertebra. When the center of gravity is aligned with *tanden*, the efficiency of your movement is maximized, minimizing fatigue.

EXERCISE FOR YOUR LIMBS

Moving Your Arms

When you contract the muscles of the little fingers, your elbows will be drawn to the sides of your body, allowing internal energy to flow along the central axis of your body.

In contract, when you contract the muscles of your thumbs, your elbows will move away from the sides of your body, allowing internal energy to glow outward. This will create stiffness in your shoulders, causing shoulder-ache. Moreover, your heels will point outward, making it difficult to utilize the body's energy efficiently. Therefore it is important to contract the muscles of your little fingers rather than your thumbs.

Moving Your Legs

Stabilize your body by allowing your weight to fall onto the ball of your foot and lowering your hips slightly.

When moving you legs, your weight should be shifted inward. If the muscles of your little toes stiffen, your knees will become unstable, making your hips shaky and prone to injury.

During exercise, in terms of the upper limbs, the muscles of the little fingers should be tightened; in terms of the lower limbs, the muscles of the big toes should be tightened. If your shoe soles show signs of excessive wear on the outer edge, this means that you body's energy is flowing outward. This should be fixed. To maintain body balance while walking, slightly lower your hips and allow the foot to naturally gravitate towards the ground.

Shi-sei

About Skeletal Structure

The center of the bone structure is located in the spinal column, which is supported by the pelvis. The hips are the foundation of all body movements. Misalignment of the spinal column can give rise to various ailments. Overuse of your arms or legs can misshape the spinal column.

Tension in muscles can result in a buildup of fatigue, which can cause minor stiffness in muscles.

Pain in the torso results from strained muscles, which are caused by distortion of the spine. When the spine is misaligned, surrounding nerves and blood vessels are compressed, producing harmful effects on the internal organs.

The pelvis of a right-handed person tends to slant rightward whereas the pelvis of a left-handed person tens to slant leftward. In a right-handed person, the left side of the body tends to shrink while the right side of the body tends to stretch. Furthermore, the left hip joint area may slide backward and outward, leading to stiffness in the left groin and knee. As a result, problems may occur in those areas. The left chest tends to become larger than the right, causing stiffness in the left shoulder. Moreover, the left leg may become slightly shorter and slide upward, causing misalignment of the pelvis. These factors can give rise to various physical symptoms. The reverse is true for a left-handed person.

Treatment that is solely focused on effected areas without any consideration for the general condition of the body can succeed only temporarily, unable to prevent the same from recurring. Make sure to pay attention to the general condition of your health to achieve a complete recovery. It is important to treat your body in its entirety.

IMPORTANCE OF BODY BALANCE

Body movement occurs according to the principle of action and counter-action, with all motions originating in *shi-ten* (a base or support point). The closer *shi-ten* is to the center of the body, the higher the efficiency. During exercise, all internal energy should be channeled into the center of the body. The purpose of tensing the muscles of *tanden* is to avoid body imbalance by focusing your energy on the center of the body. If the center of gravity does not coincide with the center of your body, your movements will be inefficient, resulting in fatigue and imbalance.

To correct distortion of your body, relax and avoid overwork. When your body feels stiff, do not overstrain yourself. To maintain your health, focus on natural and comfortable movement during a workout. Do not try to forcibly move injured parts of the body. An unhealthy lifestyle has detrimental effects on the state of your mind and body.

The legs play a pivotal role in body movement. If your legs are not stable, the balance of the entire body will be disturbed.

While walking, focus your attention on the *soku-shin*, which is located between the root of the big toe and the arch of the foot. The right way of walking is to distribute force evenly throughout the underside of your foot.

Normally, the greatest pressure is extended on the hind part of your foot, especially on the outer edge, causing the shoe sole to wear down in this area.

A person whose shoe shows signs of wear at the tip tends to be impatient. A person whose shoe shows signs of wear at the heel tends to be slow. A person whose attitude does not change even if the tip of his shoe has worn down has considerable experience.

Inability to move one's toes can restrict the movement of the entire body. Take care of your feet as they play a crucial role in body movement.

Evaluating the Condition of Your Legs
1. Move the joints of your arms, legs, knees, and elbows.
2. Check your collarbones, breastbones, ribs, chest, spine, head, and cervical vertebra.
3. Flex and extend your knees, rotate your feet, and check the pressure and tension in the joints.

During this evaluation, pay attention to the following:
Which part of the body is inflexible? Try to identify the problem by moving the affected area in different directions and various angles. After the evaluation, move the affected area in a direction that does not cause discomfort for 10 repetitions. It is important that you acquire the ability to discern the true nature of reality. This ability can be developed through training.

Maintaining Balance Through Training
The aim of training is to widen the scope of exercise through maintenance of balance.

During a warm-up exercise, whenever you feel that an activity is causing you discomfort, try an activity that makes you feel relaxed. By doing this, your exercise alternates between discomfort and relaxation. This principle should not be forgotten.

A Master's Balance

A master is fully aware of the importance of balance. A master's reign comes to an end when he dies. A master cannot make every pupil an expert. Likewise, not every pupil is worthy of succeeding his master. Understanding the interaction between respiration, food and drink, and mind and body holds the key to unlock a master's secrets. A pupil must be able to discreetly learn the secrets from his master.

Exhalation

A fast motion should take place while exhaling or holding your breath. If you move during inhalation, the balance of your body will be disturbed. In martial arts, it is important that you attack your opponent while you exhale. Your opponent's unexpected move always occurs precisely at the moment when you start to breathe in.

The ability to make judgment and take action, athletic performance, mood, and sexual prowess all depend on proper breathing with *tanden*.

Body movements should occur during exhalation. A rule of thumb is to inhale quickly and exhale slowly. To ensure success, attack your opponent while he breathes in.

Breathing with *tanden* allows you to control your body. It keeps the center of gravity low and helps to stabilize your body. Moreover, keeping *chushinten* in the hips steady can increase your physical strength. Since breathing with the chest makes it difficult to control your body, it should be avoided.

Tan-den

NATURAL BODY MOVEMENT

When the muscles of your hips are relaxed, your entire body slackens. The hips play a pivotal role in adjusting the intensity of body movement.

Moving Your Right Arm

When moving your right arm, shift your weight to the left foot to provide physical comfort. When stooping to pick up something on the floor, a right-handed person should slide his left leg forward to maintain balance. This will prevent injury as well. A left-handed person should do the opposite.

Bending Your Upper Body to the Left

When bending your upper body to the left, shifting your weight to the left foot destabilizes you body. Make sure to shift your weight to the right foot.

Do the opposite when bending your upper body to the right.

Bending Your Body

When bending your body, shift your weight in the opposite direction.

When stretching your body, shift your weight in the direction of the movement.

When leaning forward, push your buttocks out to the back.

When leaning backward, push your abdomen out to the front.

When twisting your body, shift your weight in the direction of the movement.

Shifting the Center of Gravity

When you assume a fighting stance or move your body, the center of gravity naturally shifts. If this shift does not occur, your movement will be awkward.

BOOK THREE

STRATEGY OF A VIRTUOUS MAN

To achieve something, one has to have a clear picture of how his endeavor will start and end. A leader's words and deeds can change the organization and people, which may unite or disintegrate, or rise and fall under his leadership.

A *kunishi* (virtuous man) must have the skills to communicate his feelings and be able to observe the true nature of things. He is a man who is able to find a path that is satisfactory to others. The right path is paved by the deliberate actions of people. It will vanish if you let nature take its own course. One has a duty to prevent the path from disappearing. Likewise, a house will fall apart if you allow nature to take its own course.

Let fate take care of misfortunes, work hard, and devote oneself to a task. Such is the right path.

Shobu

Chapter 1

Hints for Leaders

During Turbulent Periods

During turbulent periods, traditional powers and emerging powers engage in fierce competition. Among the traditional powers, there was a force that survived by keeping their battles to a minimum and a force that was discarded. Among the emerging powers, there was a force that emerged as an initiator but they were too early for a revolution. They became victims of the emerging era. Another force in the emerging powers was those who emerged after the time of war and became heroes by taking a leadership in history. The turbulent period was good for emerging power and emerging power. The heroes who ended the turbulent period had two things in common. One was not to make a complete conversion at a stretch and the other was not to rush.

Hints for Leaders

Who was the leader during the turbulent period?

A leader during the turbulent period had to have vitality and be a big enough person to make a historical and effective decision in split-seconds when their numbers were up. They had to have the capacity to make a quick decision. There are two conditions to be a decision maker. You have the authority to make a decision and you have to be supported by the fellowship. The most important thing for innovators is to have intuition and the ability to see your opponent's weaknesses with your own eyes.

How to Become a Leader

If you want to become a true leader, you have to know how to get on in the world as an individual and know the strategies and tactics as a part of organization. However, even if you know both of these, you are still not a mighty kind in this world because you have to assume that your opponent has also leaned all the skills they need. You can fight without knowing techniques but you can never win against a person who knows techniques. You cannot become a master even when you learn all the techniques.

You need to have a talent. It is all about knowing your own capacity.

Strength and Weakness

Everyone has weaknesses. You need to focus on improving your strengths rather than worrying about weaknesses. Defining your strengths and sharpening them is the fastest way to grow. It is important to pre-establish your expertise that you can be absolutely greater than your opponent. Don't ever show your weaknesses. You have to assume that everybody around you is your potential enemy. Not showing or letting them see your weaknesses also means you are seeing though your opponent's weaknesses.

Once you pull a bluff, make sure you carry through. There are two cases when you look at your weaknesses. One is when you are aware of your weaknesses and are emotionally ready for them. The other case is when you are not aware of your weaknesses. The important thing for a leader is to be aware of your own weaknesses and see through your opponent's weaknesses.

Military Genius Also has to be Political Genius

To be a leader, you have to be big enough to admire someone who has greater knowledge than you. Leaders understand that they can benefit from a wise person. You cannot misunderstand that you have to do everything and that you are the only person who can do it. You need to understand your capability and give way to someone else when something is beyond your capability. Even when an organization looks perfect, there are always weaknesses and loopholes. A person who has an ability to see these weaknesses and loopholes would become a leader during a turbulent period. A military force that is composed of one genius and hundreds of incompetent members would not be successful. They might succeed in military affairs but they would fail in political affairs. When a group of incompetents are united, it becomes a threat. It is difficult to win against an overwhelming majority of incompetents. To prevent them from becoming a threat, you have to be big enough to provide a place to live, a place to relax, a place where they can work, and status. Differentiating your people is also a good way to draw out the vigor of individuals. Give appropriate treatment to a lovable person. The structure of personnel management should be formed like a pyramid that is broadened as it goes from the top to the foot of the mountain.

A true military genius has to be a political genius.

Physiology of Fight

As long as people are in a society or an organization, a fight is inevitable. To win a fight, the conditions for measures and self-actualization are necessary. To fulfill the conditions, you need to study all angles of the physiology of fight. When you need to run, your objectives have to be to gain advantageous terms and time for a crucial moment. To win a fight, you have to keep growing and be strict with yourself. As a leader, it is important that you always have a lot of drive, make highly motivated preparations, develop it and promote growth.

To Become an Accomplished Leader

When you are in a situation where your sense of personal dignity is undermined or your benefit is unfairly damaged due to an irrational persecution, you need to stand up bravely, even if you are alone. You have to pull yourself up by your own bootstraps. That is how an accomplished person or an accomplished leader should be.

To become an accomplished leader, you have to be always ready for any battles.

You have to be kierinka in diplomacy. Kierinka refers to a careful individual, who pays attention to even the smallest details.

You and your organization have to be integrated.

You must not bring disgrace on your lord in diplomacy.

You need to understand that to win a battle is to bring a larger malignancy than losing.

Educational Training

The first step of managing your subordinate is to educate. The effective method to spread educational training in a group of people is geometrical progression. This method is more effective than educating all the group members together at once. Make them learn basic techniques so that they can manage the situation in response to changes.

Elite Minority

Minority cannot win against majority. However, there is a way for a minority to win. Majority sometimes lets their guard down. To catch them off guard, surprise attack is effective. This creates a possibility of minority to win against majority. For a surprise attack, you need elite minority. To benefit from surprise attack, attack individuals, deceive the opponents, take advantage of the opponents, employ a strategy as if you are hunting with a roundabout approach, and ask for necessary help, and escape from the opponents. Remember that you can practice deception.

Accomplished Leader and Ordinary Leader

The secret of becoming a winner of life is to win before you fight.

An accomplished leader has a deep consideration and a clear vision for winning before he starts fighting. So he almost always wins.

An ordinary leader starts fighting based on his emotions and intuition but without careful thoughts. He thinks about how to win after the war has started.

No Feat of Arms for Accomplished Leaders

Using armed forces is not the best thing—forgetting about armed forces is the best thing. Even when you have a powerful military force, what is important is to save the strength of the military force in a war and maintain the strong military capability. War is an act of national importance. War is a life-or-death matter for citizens and puts the existence of the country at stake. You have to give careful consideration. The most important role for a truly accomplished leader is to make other countries' leaders think that you are the leader of the country; they had better not launch an offensive against your country. There is no feat of arms for a truly accomplished leader.

Tactics

1. The best way to win against your worst enemy is to plunge them into a situation where they cannot exercise their full capability.
2. Before using armed forces, isolate the opponent country by making their associated countries secede from them. Make them lose their fighting spirit. When they do not lose their fighting spirit, use armed forces and attack their military force. This must be limited to an unavoidable situations.

3. When you launch an offensive, attack the place where the defense is weak and catch them off guard.

4. Get the first attack. Go to the battlefield before enemies and wait for them in an advantageous position. This way, you can battle with your full capability to win. Accomplished leaders, who know how important it is to get the first attack, select the timing, site, and method for the battle and force the opponent to adjust to their pace. They would not fall into someone else's pace.

5. Making a critical attack on a castle or a country has to be the last thing. It is actually better not to attack on a castle or a country. It is a waste of time and military force.

6. When you put too much pressure on the opponent, they start busting a gut and it will cause you trouble with handling them. If you drove them up a wall, leave them an escape route and lower their guard. Then you can make another attack.

7. When you plan a strategy, make sure you attack their weak points and deal with them at their lower condition not their innate ability.

8. Plan for establishment and maintenance.
   Which is more difficult between establishment and maintenance?
   Bogenrei: "Establishment is more difficult."
   Gicho: "To sustain what you have once established is more difficult. Therefore, maintenance is more difficult."

After hearing their opinions, Taiso answered "Both Bogenrei and I underwent hard times to establish the country. Those who fought together know how difficult it is to establish a nation. However, once a nation is built, it is already a history. The most difficult thing from now on is to protect the nation. Therefore, we should focus on the maintenance of our country."

Jo-hoh

CHAPTER 2

Four Types of Information Strategy

People consume information like food. If presented with convincing facts, a repulsive story can be transformed into an appealing story. Information strategy can be divided into four categories: logical, straightforward, calculating, and combination.

Logical Strategist
* Attempts to force others to obey him through his logic.
* Reaches a conclusion without taking other people's opinions into consideration.
* Is unable to understand the mentality of other cultures. Experiences difficulty adapting to a new way of life in a different culture.
* Lacks a sense of humor.
* Because emphasis is placed on rational thinking, information provided by a logical strategist is not deceptive. However, such information may contain erroneous interpretation.
* A logical strategist relies on a conventional strategy, applying the same method to different cases. The apparatus for propaganda is fully established.

Straightforward Strategist
* Values speed and objectivity, making full use of newspapers and other medium to deliver his message.
* Invests heavily in the development of a large-scale network.
* Emphasizes factual reporting.
* Campaigns vigorously when the tide is running in his direction, but becomes silent when the tide is turning against him.
* Is inclined to express his true feelings. May publicly express his delight when winning a battle or show obvious contempt for his opponents.

* Is unable to understand the feelings of peoples from different cultures.
* Tends to be overly sensitive to domestic relations.
* Is unable to differentiate between facts and propaganda. Is weak in tactical maneuvering
* Is not competent in the area of counterintelligence
* Lacks the ability to outmaneuver his opponents.

Calculating Strategist

* Information is disseminated in a question-and-answer format. A calculating strategist urges the citizens of an enemy country to arrive at their own conclusions.
* Emphasizes reporting that appears to emotion rather than reason. However, if his opponents value rationality, a calculating strategist will place greater emphasis on logic.
* Remains unruffled even in adverse circumstances. Is bold enough to disseminate information that can jeopardize his country. Wins the trust of his enemies through factual reporting, only to betray them at the end by circulating disinformation.
* Believes that in order to succeed in propaganda, one must be assimilated into the enemy's culture.
* Spends money generously and relies on the select few.
* Invests heavily in devising a plan to launch an all-out attack on the enemy when convinced that such an attack will be effective.
* Knows the importance of information strategy in warfare. Needs assistance from those who are brilliant at influencing other people through their rhetoric and articulateness. Information manipulation is often used by nations that have been in constant conflict with neighboring ethnic groups for centuries. These nations are knowledgeable about the mental attitudes of other ethnic groups.

Combination Strategist

* Is similar to a calculating strategist.
* Launches a media campaign directed at the general public, which is intended to provoke emotional reactions.
* This campaign appears to the audience's personal interests.
* This campaign is conducted insidiously and cunningly.

* Resorts to psychological tactics that are aimed at perplexing the enemy.

Psychological tactics on a worldwide scale are often deployed by powerful nations even in time of peace to discreetly advance their own agenda.

Politics and Ethics
Politics has nothing to do with ethics. Those who do not know this fact will perish. Politics is all about deception and scheming. A lie told by a warrior is called a ploy and a lie told by a saint is a white lie. Justify your lie to win the battle. This is how you survive in warfare.

Tradition
Tradition must be transmitted from generation to generation; otherwise, it will disappear. Harmony makes it possible to preserve tradition. The old is constantly being replaced by the new and this regeneration keeps the old tradition alive, albeit in a different form. Everything comes to an end when this regeneration process stops.

BOOK FOUR

HOW TO INTERPRET YOUR MIND

To accomplish a big task, do not neglect small matters and work hard. A great achievement is an accumulation of small deeds. An unwise person, hoping to achieve something big, pays no attention to small things and frets over the fact that he is making little progress.

We are all destined to die. Life is an unexpected gift. Be aware of the fact that we are lucky to be alive today.

The world is like an ocean. There are three basic things you need to do to cross this ocean, i.e. the world: produce food, clothing, and shelter; make full use of that food, clothing, and shelter without being wasteful; and extend help to others. People are worried about wealth and poverty, and joy and sorrow. However, whether or not you can survive in the world is determined by your swimming skills.

It is said that in order to achieve a state of *satori* (spiritual enlightenment), one must first be immersed in the world of life and death and lustful desire. We are included to judge others based on our own viewpoints and capabilities. Interpreting facts conveniently will make us blind to the truth.

Kun-shi

Oscillation stems from our inability to see the truth, and our thoughts are bound by constant cravings. As a result, we end up ruining our personal relationships with others. Such cravings, anger, and foolishness are called *san-doku* (three poisons). Peace of mind can be attained by eliminating these poisons from our mind. Suffering results when we perceive something as painful. In other words, the state of our mind determines whether or not we experience suffering. When we observe the world with the wisdom of *ku* (emptiness), which is a concept of *hannya* (*prajna*), your mind will be liberated from suffering.

The purpose of self-cultivation lies in the development of positive attitudes, with emphasis on understanding the value and meaning of suffering rather than obliterating suffering. Avarice makes our personality weak, and consequently, wisdom and hope will be lost. Defilement of our mind leads to loss of our character. Learning is not to understand with one's head, rather, it is to understand with one's body.

QUALITIES A VIRTUOUS MAN MUST POSSESS

A virtuous man:

* Acknowledges the need to secure people's cooperation.
* Possesses the flexibility and sensitivity to leave room for others to deliberate.
* Takes an open-minded approach to new ideas without adhering to conventional methods.
* Can control his anger even when things did not go as planned.
* Is not arrogant or lazy.
* Has the skill to eliminate feelings of resentment, hostility, and alienation.
* Frequently evaluates his subordinates' performance and acts in a fair manner.
* Knows that people will unleash their full potential when they are motivated by their own interests.
* Knows the following facts and how to deal with them: People tend to resist new things. Resistance entails change. Change entails disorder, and vice versa.
* Is aware of the fact that people hate to be given orders.

A VIRTUOUS MAN CAN EMPATHIZE WITH OTHERS

Not all thoughts are expressed verbally. Be able to read a person's real intentions hidden behind his words.

Oftentimes, you may not notice people's reluctance to accept your feelings or actions. Be aware of this fact.

We have a tendency to hear what we want to hear, focus on what we want to say, and fail to make sure that we really understand what others are saying. Be aware of this tendency.

Be willing to give others opportunities to express their thoughts, and listen to them attentively.

Know the fact that the most important part of a discussion is to make others understand your point.

A VIRTUOUS MAN IS CONSIDERATE TOWARD OTHERS

A virtuous man should strive to change the way he behaves.

He should listen to what others have to say.

In the decision making process, a virtuous man should include everyone in order to reach an agreement.

A virtuous man should act in a way that shows consideration for others.

QUALITIES A VIRTUOUS MAN SHOULD AVOID

* An overbearing authoritarian who exerts power.
* A supervisor who cannot communicate effectively with his subordinates.
* A person who lacks spontaneity.
* A supervisor whose subordinates cover up their mistakes.
* A supervisor whose subordinates harbor hostile feelings.
* A supervisor whose subordinates rise up in revolt.
* A person who creates a repressive organizational environment.
* A person who is too straightforward and does not realize that revealing one's real intentions can be risky. A person who opens up too easily.

DUTIES OF A VIRTUOUS MAN

A virtuous man should:

* Think about what he can do to contribute to society before taking action.
* Think about what he should be expecting.
* Be able to deal with situations on a case-by-case basis, taking into considerations what goal and task he wishes to achieve.
* Assign subordinates a clear mission and encourage them to accomplish their mission.
* Create an environment where subordinates can feel that their efforts to achieve their goal are enjoyable and rewarding.
* Hold a meeting to respond to change, modification, and growth.
* Seek prior consent from others in the course of an action. By laying such groundwork, the impact of transition, opposition, and emotional reaction will be mitigated.
* Support subordinates in a way that motivates them.

Wa

A Desirable Organization for a Virtuous Man

This organization is one:

* That can respond to circumstantial changes.
* That nurtures a satisfactory relationship between supervisors and subordinates.
* That strives to cultivate the competence, skill, and talent of the members.
* That brings out productivity and development.
* Where the decisions are made by creative and talented personnel.

* That emphasizes education and training. Training that focuses on learning of basics through knowledge; education based on dissemination of knowledge.
* Where supervisors and subordinates fulfill their responsibilities.
* That is responsive to suggestions.
* Where supervisors are insightful and willing to take action.
* That implements good proposals.
* That can make decisions without hesitation when opportunities come.
* That can rectify its weaknesses.
* That treats people with respect and courtesy.
* That grapples with issues steadfastly and has the ability to deliver results.

WHAT IS THE WISE MAN'S ATTITUDE?

If you have a thought that you are doing something for others, you start blaming the person and even holding a grudge. A wise man knows that it is better to believe that you are doing something for yourself.

A wise man knows a small trust can make a great confidence.

A wise man's attitude should be frank in action and word. The modifier obstructs the efficacy, and knows to forget about the essence.

BOOK FIVE

WORDS AND DEEDS OF A VIRTUOUS MAN

THE WORDS AND DEEDS OF A RESPONSIBLE
PERSON ARE TACTICAL

Conversation requires techniques. For example, you should listen to the other person attentively and be able to anticipate where a conversation is going. There are a number of ways to ask questions and carry on a conversation.

Your words sound convincing when you have confidence in yourself. On the contrary, the power of your words diminishes when you try to manipulate the other party. Speaking hysterically will provoke fear in the other person.

It is a challenge to persuade someone who harbors hostility toward you. Convincing such a person is impossible without making an effort to develop positive feelings toward the person and remove hostility. To persuade the other party in a conversation, sympathize with him after identifying and understanding his personality and mentality.

Compliments

Compliments are an effective means to save face and maintain friendships. Compliments should be used effectively.

Those who lack persuasive skills are often reluctant to understand others and are self-absorbed.

We tend to judge someone through colored glasses when meeting the person for the first time. Many of us cannot look at a person in his true light. Those with psychological problems are more likely to make such mistakes. It is important to pay attention to a person's true character and confirm what you have found with your heart and eyes.

When meeting someone, concentrate your mind and be mentally ready.
Your mind should be fully prepared as if you are going to a battleground. Remain mentally calm and relaxed, and try to make the first move and take the initiative while being cordial.

Those who are mentally immature lack the ability to discern the true nature of people.
Those who are psychologically unsound are discontent with everything. Exercise moderation when you act and speak.

I-Shiki

WORDS AND AWARENESS OF A VIRTUOUS MAN

No success can be achieved without professional attitudes and determination. To be a professional, you should be able to enjoy what you do without being obsessive.

Whatever you enjoy doing make your profession. As a result, things will go more smoothly.

Be careful in your speech and conduct so as to gain people's support and achieve success. No one can succeed without professionalism and resoluteness. God will offer help only when you possess these qualities. Words can be both good and evil.

BASIC KNOWLEDGE ABOUT LANGUAGE (DIALOGUE)

A dialogue involves listening, use of language, emotions, desires, opposition, speech, action, and questioning. How you conduct yourself determines your relationship with others.

How to Listen

When listening, be silent and show the other party that you are paying attention by using eye contact, giving responses, and gesturing. Confirm what the other person is saying.

Choice of Words

Choose active words and phrases that make favorable impressions and win sympathy. Some examples of these are "I care about you," "I understand your position," "You do not need to worry about it."

Expressing Emotions

Words that express negative feelings and attitudes will deteriorate your personal relations.

Negative Feelings

When trying to pacify an upset person, ask him what makes him upset. If what the other person says or does is unbearable, tell him frankly how you feel.

When You Do Not Want to Hear Something

Excuse yourself by telling the person that you will listen to him when your mind is not occupied.

How to Satisfy a Person's Desire

Give them an opportunity to talk and resolve differences.

How to Deal with Opposition

Do your best to understand the other person's position and allow him to explain his standpoint.

Positive Behavior

Try to behave in a positive way.

Negative Mind

People lie to themselves when they are overcome by fear. Being oversensitive to signs of failure drives you to feel self-contempt. Self-contempt will only foster the feeling of regret.

Associating With Someone with Negative Attitudes

Avoid associating with people who have negative attitudes.

How to Transform Negative Thought Into Positive Ones

Believe in your worthiness as a person.

Be yourself. Being yourself means that there is no need to compare yourself to others, show yourself off, worry about how others perceive you, or pretend to be someone else. Being yourself has no harmful effects on you. The most important thing you can do for yourself is to be yourself.

Know others. A mentally mature person enjoys knowing other people. A self-centered person feels it is painful to be generous to others; oftentimes such a person lacks empathy and compassion and is dissatisfied with himself. Moreover, such a person is not often aware that he is responsible for people's reactions to his words and actions and he should be able to predict such reactions. To get to know someone, acknowledge the fact that each person has a different personality. This will enable you to react and predict in a proper way.

Whom Should You Associate With?
A considerate and warm-hearted person.
A person who follows the path of righteousness.
Find someone who is trustworthy and sincere.
A person who does not lie.
A courageous person.
Find someone who has the ability to devise a strategy and is persevering in his efforts to solve a problem.

MEN AND WOMEN TALK DIFFERENTLY

Men's talk tends to focus on self-assertion, self-esteem, and contention. When conversing with a man, women should not say something that will hurt his self-esteem.

Women relieve their frustration by talking. Women's talk tends to center on topics that evoke harmony and sympathy. When conversing with a woman, men should show sympathy, give feedback, and listen attentively.

Kai-wa

Ten Requirements for a Productive Meeting

The purpose of a meeting is to solve a problem and to convey information.

At a meeting, what will be discussed and who will lead the discussion should be decided.

Once such decisions are made, the focus should be shifted to the matter in question. Discuss whether there is room for improvement and identify the real problems. Review potential solutions that can be implemented effectively and discuss their possible consequences. Assign a person to be a leader, and decide what should be done to tackle the problem, who will be involved, when and where the process should take place, and when it should be completed.

The meeting should proceed in a positive and supportive atmosphere. Avoid coercive words and critical attitudes. When making a request, ask politely if anything can be done to be of help.

Every unsolved problem involving individuals, groups, recommendations, and research should be dealt with. Do not leave problems unsolved.

If certain issues are not resolved, another meeting should be held to address them.

Once the course of actions is decided, it should be followed through responsibly. The details of the meeting should remain confidential. A copy of the decisions made at the meeting should be distributed to the attendees.

Form a project team consisting of at least five people, with one person in charge of the team.

Attendees should not attempt to dominate, monopolize, or disrupt the meeting.

A system should be in place that allows opinions and reports to flow smoothly from top to bottom and vice versa.

BOOK SIX

STRATEGY OF THE MIND

Everyone has a different personality. Along with the environment each individual is surrounded with, both genetic factors and acquired factors have a huge impact on personalities. Write down the most fundamental things you learned from your elders.

Shoh-nen

Balancing Your Mind

Personalities vary widely, and each personality has its weaknesses. There are ways to distinguish and predict traits of a personality, and to analyze a person's wavelengths, perspectives, and thoughts. Out predecessors surreptitiously mastered the techniques of mind reading and kept them secret. These mind reading techniques have eventually evolved into today's psychology. Once you are familiar with a person's characteristics, you should analyze a wide range of factors such as dispositions, functions, comparisons, *yin* and *yang* (negative and positive) qualities, and wavelengths to judge his character.

How to Keep Your Balance of Mind

Each personality comes with flaws. These flaws can be removed by keeping your mind well balanced; this means that intellect, reason, instinct, and emotion must be balanced out with each other.

Figure: The Balanced Mind

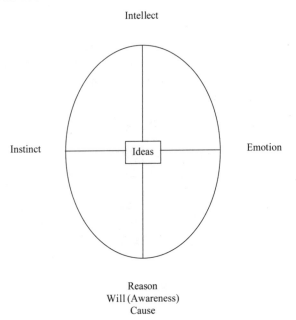

At the center of the circle are ideas. To maintain the balance of the mind, the circle must be equally divided into intellect, reason, instinct, and emotion. It is important that the mind is focused on the center.

When reason and emotion are emphasized, stress and irritability increase.

When the functions of intellect and reason weaken, it will be difficult to properly assess or judge others. This results because instinct and emotion are enhanced.

On the contrary, stronger intellect and reason will result in a lack of flexibility and excessive assertiveness.

Heightened instinct and emotion lead to an inability to properly judge

he other person. This happens because intellect and reason are not func-
ioning well.

By focusing your mind on the center, you will be able to control your
deas, which are formed by five *kyu* (cause), will, and awareness.

The mind can be roughly divided into three parts: the mind of a child,
he mind of an adult, and the mind of a parent. These three minds are mutu-
lly related and interact with each other to form one's psyche. The mind of
child is the source of all energy. Emotions such as sympathizing, being
n wonder, and crying arise from this mind. It controls a person's emo-
ional aspects, disciplines, efforts, and expectations. The mind of an adult
nalyzes the cause of failure and governs one's actual life. The mind of a
arent controls one's ethical aspects.

HOW TO DISTINGUISH DIFFERENT PERSONALITIES

'ersonalities can be classified into four main types:

- Egocentric Type
- Unctuous Type
- Logical Type
- Conformist Type

The Egocentric Type

An egocentric person is a man of action, but tends to ignore the opinions
f others. To make up for this shortcoming, such a person should repeat the
ther person's main points and listen intently during a conversation.

The Unctuous Type

An unctuous person is cheerful and lively, but tends to be thoughtless. Such
person should come up with alternative ideas and use words that can win
he trust of others.

The Logical Type

A logical person is cautious, but tends to be emotionless. Such a person
hould use words that show sympathy for others.

The Conformist Type

A conformist is easily swayed by the opinions of others. Such a person is good at accepting the suggestions of others, but this trait causes him to be stressed out. One of his faults is that he cannot think for himself. Such a person should use words that express feelings.

CHARACTERISTICS OF THE FOUR FUNCTIONS OF THE MIND

The functions of the mind can be classified into four categories: logic, emotion, sensation, and intuition.

The logical category tends to think rationally and logically. It is poor at expressing one's feelings. It is not polished in aesthetic aspects, such as clothing.

The emotional category acts on emotion rather than logic. Such a mind tends to judge matters according to one's own criteria of values regarding what is right and wrong and appropriate and inappropriate. This person can accurately assess the value of things and judge people. In conversation, phrases such as "you should" and "you ought to" are used to impose one's values on others. This person also has a tendency to lose track of one's thoughts.

The sensory category is passionate, pragmatic, and realistic. He values experience, listens attentively, and enjoys listening to others. He is also particular about taste, and likes things that stimulate the senses. This type of person tends to overindulge in sexual pleasure. He is also worldly, practical, and conservative.

The intuitive category tends to be academic and idealistic. They like to plan ahead, are future-oriented, and have the ability to foresee new opportunities. Someone of this type tends to be self-righteous and lack steadfastness.

Ka-chi

How to Classify Personalities According to Contrastive Qualities

There are five categories of contrastive qualities: spontaneous and reactive, intuitive and sensory, perceptive and judgmental, introverted and extroverted, and emotional and logical.

Characteristics of Spontaneous and Reactive Personalities

A spontaneous type of person is full of vitality and thinks rationally. They tend to think and act on one's own.

In contrast, the reactive type lacks vitality and is not mentally active. They tend to overreact to stimulants and get angry easily. Since a hot-tempered person is lacking in deep emotion, he should try to be in contact with Mother Nature. Moreover, such a person should enjoy music and do some exercise to vent his anger. Quick-tempered people should take good care of their liver.

Characteristics of Intuitive and Sensory Personalities

The intuitive type puts emphasis on one's intuition. They are imaginative and idealistic, but at the same time, tend to be reserved. This person likes to drink alone in a lonely setting. In terms of strategy, this personality type tends to focus on winning short-term battles. He is wordy in his writing and describes his feelings rather than facts in a diary. This personality is also inclined to speak repetitiously. It is believed that this type of person excels in psychology, literature and art.

Conversely, the sensory type likes to use the five senses to perceive things. They are realistic, outgoing, and are sensitive to external stimulants. The sensory type analyzes objectively and reaches a decision after careful consideration. They are decisive. This person likes to drink in a social setting. In terms of strategy, this person tends to focus on winning a long term battle. They write briefly and concisely, and describe facts in a diary. This person also focuses on the main points when talking. It is said that this type of person is proficient in the fields of law and technology.

Characteristics of Perceptive and Judgmental Personalities

The perceptive type takes external circumstances into consideration when thinking about something. They value experience, and like to adapt themselves to the environment. They are easygoing.

The judgmental type, however, likes to influence the environment when making a decision. They like to decide based on their own will. This person likes to have the final say, even on trivial matters.

Characteristics of Introverted and Extroverted Personalities

The introverted type is quiet and modest and tends to be reticent. They like to focus attention on the inner world. This personality type is committed to its tasks and has strong beliefs. They persevere and have the ability to concentrate.

The extroverted type is inclined to act hastily before careful consideration. This person seeks external stimuli and is interested in his surroundings. Sociable and active, this person is talkative and open about his feelings.

Characteristics of Emotional and Logical Personalities

The emotional type is warmhearted. They respect the feelings of others when dealing with something, and they are likely to make decisions based on their likes and dislikes.

On the other hand, the logical type thinks rationally. He constructs his arguments based on logic and makes decisions after objective analysis and assessment.

How to Classify Personalities Based on the Principle of *Yin* and *Yang*

Tai-In (big *yin*) is humble and gentle on the surface. He does not show his true feelings on his face. This person tends to be insidious and greedy and is an opportunist.

Sho-in (small *yin*) is coldhearted and unwilling to help others. This person craves things that belong to others and takes delight in watching others suffer.

Tai-yo (big *yang*) often boasts about themselves despite their incompetence. This person is unapologetic about their failure and tends to blame others for their mistakes.

Sho-yo (small *yang*) acts cautiously. They are full of conceit and behave with an air of self-importance when holding a managerial position.

Characteristics of a Person with Balanced *Yin* and *Yang*

This person behaves with composure and remains humble despite high status. They are benevolent and win the admiration of others with their benevolence. This person goes along with the natural forces and is at peace with himself. Considerate towards others, this person is fearless and can restrain feelings of joy and always handle matters in a calm manner.

BOOK SEVEN

THE LAW OF ANGER AND THE LAW OF SNAPPING

CHAPTER 1

Managing and Understanding the Mind

The martial arts are profound and difficult. Having similar experiences, undergoing the same training, reading similar books, eating the same food, and seeing, hearing, and experiencing the same phenomena will not produce the same reactions in different individuals. Rather, each person will interpret his experiences differently. Those who are following the right path should spare no effort to acquire the ability to make sound judgments.

Our predecessors have taught us the importance of practicing moderation in our daily lives and the danger of seeking fleeting pleasure. The goal is to find a higher and more distant path.

The purpose of physical training is to pay meticulous attention to one's body from head to toe, being mindful of the capillaries that cover the entire body.

Life is full of adversities. There is a time when your education, social status, fame, fortune, and the family ties that you have established over the years will become useless. At a decisive moment like this, you must concentrate on your duties and channel all your efforts into following the right path. Perseverance, hope, creativity, and optimism will eventually regain trust and love of others, leading to the rebirth of your soul.

To develop and nurture virtues, you must show sincerity in word and deed. The bigger the obstacles, the greater the virtues you will develop.

To understand the sacred emptiness (*ku*), you must follow the right path without being distracted by the concept of *ku*, your intellect, mind, body, or skill. Once all earthly desires and everything else are dispelled from your mind, you will be able to achieve completeness in mind, body, and intellect.

Cho-wa

MANAGING THE MIND

Arrogance

Arrogance disorients you. Arrogant attitudes are sometimes seen in monks, scholars, and even poets. Arrogance is usually accompanied by insecurity. Arrogance arises from one's desire to reap undeserved rewards and to navigate through life with little difficulty. The ultimate goal of learning is to practice what one has learned. One must act for the benefit of others through self-effacement. To find the right path, action should be taken without being swayed by your selfish desires. Arrogant attitudes can be corrected by straightening your mind, controlling your body, and fostering harmony among people.

Suffering

Anger, fear, greed, poverty, foul language, discontent, and confusion not only give rise to suffering but also undermine one's health. Indecisiveness, trepidation, skepticism, and laziness will result in failure. Self-centeredness arouses anxiety and wickedness in one's mind, creating enemies. An ignorant person, who is incapable of learning from his experiences, cannot attain wisdom. When great dreams are fulfilled, lofty ideals will be achieved. Failure brings you one step closer to glory, which is built upon bravery, faith, hardship, and elimination of desire. Divine intentions will be revealed to those who gain a complete understanding of the mind.

Concentration

To elevate the mind to a higher level, focus on the task before you without being distracted by feelings of dissatisfaction.

You can improve yourself by achieving independence and stability, which will make it possible to acquire knowledge, spirituality, and competence.

Problems will disappear as soon as the undesirable behavior is rectified. The ultimate power derives from *fudo-shin* and the ability to concentrate. Concentration is possible only when your mind is at peace.

To purify your mind, try to understand your true feelings and reflect on your deeds. Mental strength can enrich one's life; mental acuity can change the course of one's life. When one's actions are dictated by one's conscience, the power of concentration, and *fudo-shin*, true contentment will be found and there will be no regret.

Those who shape their own destiny know that if they continue to do their best, unfavorable circumstances will be followed by favorable circumstances. They are aware that grueling training can eventually bring happiness and encourage the emergence of new skills.

The power of concentration is infinite. Concentration can be achieved only when all distractive thoughts are removed from one's mind. Elimination of earthly thoughts requires inner harmony, which will purify the mind and allow one to make sound judgments. The ability to concentrate can increase one's capability, making it possible to act widely. Perfect concentration is necessary to achieve a complete success. Perfect concentration can be realized through simplification of the thought process. When the thought process is complicated, the power of concentration will gradually diminish before accomplishing a goal. In our search for inner harmony, suffering is created and harmony becomes lost.

UNDERSTANDING THE MIND

To control the mind and attain tranquility, you must first eradicate negative thoughts from your mind. Negative ideas give rise to illusions, making it difficult to perceive reality. Furthermore, negative thoughts may provoke the urge to seek sensual and physical pleasure; consequently, you may begin to take delight in other people's misfortune and become reluctant to work hard. As a result, your mind and body will begin to have negative influences on others.

The mind becomes powerful through concentration and weak through distraction. Being generous means acting kindly toward others without expectation of repayment. The state of your mind greatly affects the choices you make in your life.

Harsh environments facilitate the development of one's ability. An irrational person lacks the capacity to control his mind. Happiness is attained when one's desires are satisfied. Material success can lock you up in a cage that prevents you from pursuing the path to truth. We will reap what we have sown. Anxiety is the enemy of the mind.

An unscrupulous person naturally attracts unscrupulous people. When held captive of your own desire, your mind becomes vulnerable and suffering is created. Those who are blinded by their selfish desires will be abandoned by their friends. Loss of sight deprives you of sound judgment and knowledge. A self-disciplined person never panics. Peaceful and fearless, he lets his conscience be his guide. A person who follows his conscience is thoughtful and is surrounded by good friends. Kind at heart, such a person possesses great dignity.

Those who endure hardships will receive help from others. Those who cling to their hopes will receive help from God. Life is a battle in which constant effort is required to receive help from God, nature, and others. Happiness in life comes from the joy of giving rather than the anguish of taking. Blessed are those who give, not those who take. Love resides in sincerity and generosity. Good deeds and words will eventually take you to paradise.

ATTITUDES OF A VIRTUOUS MAN

If you undertake a task for the benefit of others, you may start criticizing or harboring resentment against the very people you are trying to help.

Be aware that a task will become much easier if you do it for your own benefit.

Be aware that some people are willing to sacrifice their lives to defend personal honor while others are motivated by self-interest.

Be aware that accumulation of small trust will eventually lead to greater trust.

Be aware that hard work without order, discipline, or goal will bear no fruit.

Your words and deeds should not be ostentatious. Be aware that pretentiousness hampers your effort to fulfill your duty and diverts your attention from the true nature of reality.

Ika-ri

CHAPTER 2

Law of Anger and Law of Snapping

Expression of anger can be used to develop a better relationship. By communicating your anger, you can solve a problem and rebuild a relationship. However, snapping is different. To snap means to break. When you snap, you are at the point where you have no other way to let the steam go and you lose words. You are at the point where you can do nothing else but commit a violent act.

THE TYPES OF ANGER AND SNAPPING

Eruption Type: These types of people shout furiously and feel disgusted with themselves afterward.

Sarcastic Type: These types of people do not say anything but show their anger in action.

Arsonist Type: These types of people fire up people around them and do not solve problems by themselves.

Withholding Type: These types of people withhold their anger and break down. They find an outlet in people weaker than them. A good example is domestic violence. Withholding anger does not solve a problem.

Solutions

When you hurt someone you are usually insensitive. If you stay insensitive, the problem will occur again. To deal with this, you need to pause for one day to think about how the other person responded and what the problem was. When you feel anger towards someone, it is better to think overnight. When you are angry, you cannot think straight. You need to know what the cause of your anger is, otherwise, you do not even know why you are angry and you lose words. Pause for one day and think about what you want to do and what you want the other person to do. This is the way to solve a problem.

MANAGEMENT OF THE MIND

A fearful person is inwardly afraid. When driven into a corner, this person may quickly lose his composure. When attacked by a fearful person, call out someone's name loudly, pretending that someone else is present. This will improve your chance of escaping.

A calm person is composed and self-controlled. This person is experienced in combat and can make a fight or flight decision in a split second. A bag, magazine, book, or newspaper can be used as a protective shield against small weapons such as a knife.

Raku

Comfort Zone

The comfort zone is a space between you and the other person. It is an egg-shaped area and if you go into the area, the other person feels uncomfortable.

When you give someone your business card or love letter, you should not step into their comfort zone because they will feel uncomfortable. You can give it at the middle point between you and the person.

The comfort zone is oval-shaped. If you stand right next to the person, you can get closer to him without making him feel uncomfortable.

When you hand something to someone, you can go to his or her side and show it to him or her first. Then go around to the front and give it to him or her. When you are interviewing someone, you can also stand next to him or her first and then go to the front when you hold out a microphone. You can do the same thing when you pass out fliers. This way, chances are higher that people will take the flyer.

THE LAW OF MYSTERY

The law of mystery refers to the golden ratio. This is the fundamental source of beauty. The golden ration is 1:1.68. Our brain recognizes things with the golden ratio as beauty. This golden ratio is used in plastic surgery, paintings, the television screen, books, credit cards, and architecture. The ratio of 1:1.68 creates an amazing and mysterious rectangle.

BOOK EIGHT

HOW TO INTERPRET WAVELENGTHS

CHAPTER 1

How to Interpret Wavelengths

People tend to have a favorable opinion of someone who is on the same or similar wavelength as them. To win the heart of someone, look for similarities between yourself and the other person; furthermore, know the wavelength of the other person and take an appropriate approach. If the other person behaves on the same wavelength as you do, you can assume that you and the person are compatible with each other.

Ha-cho

HOW TO INTERPRET THE RELATIONSHIPS BETWEEN EYE MOVEMENTS AND THOUGHTS

Suppose that you are asking someone a question face to face. You can infer what the other person is thinking from the way he moves his eyes.

When his eyes move horizontally from side to side, he is recollecting something from obscure memory.

When his eyes move to your upper right, he is visualizing something that he has never seen before.

When his eyes move to your lower right, he is visualizing something associated with the body.

When his eyes move to your upper left, he is recalling something that he has seen before.

When his eyes move to your lower left, he is thinking of a sound or voice that he has heard before.

HOW TO INTERPRET AND WIN THE HEARTS OF OTHERS

Humans have three types of wavelengths: visual, auditory, and general sensory.

Characteristics of the Visual Type

Moves one's eyes upward. Talks fast, uses visual words, and is quick-witted. Has a taste for colorful things and likes to enjoy beautiful scenery and landscapes.

Characteristics of the Auditory Type

Moves one's eyes from side to side. Often uses words that are associated with sounds. Is full of facial expressions, and likes to debate and attend meetings. Feels at ease with oneself in a tranquil setting, like a place where the sound of waves can be heard.

Characteristics of a General Sensory Type

Moves one's eyes downward. Talks slowly and with stability. Often uses words that are associated with the body and senses. Likes things that are soothing to one's mind, and pleasant things with good texture.

To get to know people, you should tailor a conversation to each person's wavelength. If the other person behaves as you do, the conversation can be called successful.

Blinking of Eyes

It is known that there is a relationship between blinking the eyes and lying. Blinking the eyes provides important information about the other person; specifically, it can tell you whether or not he is telling the truth in response to your question. You should carefully observe the way the other person blinks and look for a pattern.

How Hormones Affect Your Mental State

Physiological and psychological problems are largely caused by the workings of the brain cells and hormones. It is important to know the functions of hormones to understand how your mind works.

Examples of Successful Communication of Love

It is said that if confession of love is done within three months after meeting the person, the success rate will go up. During that period, you should try to develop intimacy with the person. The possibility of success further increases if you tell him or her that you wish to have a committed relationship between the hours of 6PM and 11PM.

Ren-ai

ROMANCE HORMONES

We fall in love because we want to experience the pleasurable sensations produced by PEA (phenylethylamine) and endorphins. When you are in love, a hormone called PEA becomes active in the brain. This hormone can severely impair your judgment and make you blind in your romantic relationship.

PEA can also excite your brain and suppress your appetite. PEA may cause you to lose weight when you are in love. The effects of PEA can only last for three years at the longest. However, romance with obstacles tends to endure much longer.

When PEA is in action, your brain becomes excited, resulting in the release of a hormone called beta-endorphin. This hormone is involved with memory, learning, and suppression of pain. Endorphins are secreted when certain desires are aroused. Such desires include: a desire to want to know the other person, a desire for sensual pleasure, a desire to touch the other person, a sexual urge, and a yearning for further sensual pleasure. This hormone disappears quickly after it is released.

A love affair is fun. You can see your partner only when you feel like it. Marriage, on the other hand, comes with a responsibility of having to see your spouse every day even if you do not wish to see him or her.

MONOTONOUS PHASE HORMONE (SEROTONIN)

Once you are married, thanks to the successful activities of PEA and endorphin, serotonin, a hormone that causes the brain to feel at ease and happy, is activated. This hormone also represses your sexual desire, leading to the monotonous phase of marriage.

How should you deal with the dull phase of your marriage brought on by serotonin, which represses your sexual desire? First you should try to reactivate PEA and beta-endorphin. Do something that makes your brain think that you are in love. Do something that makes your heart throb with excitement. For instance, thrilling activities, such as riding a roller coaster, are recommended. Unfortunately, this is a short-term remedy and works for only a few weeks.

The following is what you can do to find your way out of the dull phase: Empathize with your spouse, alternate each other's roles, put emphasis on physical contact and touch, look into your spouse's eyes to have eye communication, and do something exciting together.

WHAT KIND OF PERSON DO YOU FALL IN LOVE WITH?

We have a tendency to fall in love with someone who has similar values and ideas and who possesses qualities that compensate for our shortcomings. For instance, a tall person may be inclined to fall in love with a shorter person.

HOW TO MAKE YOUR RELATIONSHIP LAST

Why does your relationship not last? It is because misjudgment and distortion in perception can make you overly appreciative of your partner's trivial acts of kindness. Once you come to your senses, you will realize the disparity between reality and perception. This is the time when you start thinking about divorce. Your relationship is likely to be successful if you pick a partner who shares similar values and wants to have a reciprocal relationship with you.

DIFFERENCES IN THINKING BETWEEN THE SEXES

Male

Men tend to judge something according to the person's standing on a vertical scale. For men, rationality and pride are important.

A wound to their pride can be a source of stress. Men use the cerebral cortex to think, which governs analytical and logical thoughts. It is believed that indecisiveness in men derives from the cerebral cortex. Since men analyze the reason why their heart is broken until they find a satisfactory answer, they are slow to recover. A man's brain is not well suited to handle two different tasks at once. When men are in a stressful situation, they should eat or drink something light. Chewing gum is also helpful. It is important that men feel motivated.

Female

Women put emphasis on emotions and desires. When in love, women use the limbic system, which controls intuitive and emotional thoughts. Consequently, women are more realistic and quick to recover. The source of women's meticulousness is the corpus callosum. In fact, a woman's corpus callosum is twice as big as a man's. When women fall in love, a female hormone called estrogen is activated. Subsequently their skin condition improves, resulting in firmer skin; in addition, their body shape may become slimmer. When women are under stress or heartbroken, they should ask someone to praise their good qualities.

Hei-an

Testosterone and Estrogen

Testosterone (male) is a hormone that commands motivation and leadership. Estrogen (female) gives rise to the gentle behavior of women. When estrogen is working in full force and brings out gentleness in women, secretion of testosterone is stimulated, giving motivation to men. On the contrary, if the secretion of estrogen is insufficient, men will lose their motivation and become unproductive.

HOW TO ENHANCE MEN'S SELF-CONFIDENCE

Women should eat food that helps to increase their estrogen levels. Consume two apples and 100 grams of peanuts per day. Raisins and *natto* (fermented soybeans) are also recommended.

Consciously use compliments to boost his self-confidence. Behave accordingly.

Energize the functions of the hypothalamus by stimulating appetite and desires and getting enough sleep.

Be physically affectionate, such as kissing in the morning and evening.

Strive to discover good qualities in one's partner.

CHARACTERISTICS OF A WOMAN WITH LOW ESTROGEN LEVELS

* She is stingy and reluctant to pick up the tab. She wants to have something that belongs to others.
* She cries easily due to a lack of consideration for others.

* Is spiteful and good at finding fault with others.
* Prepares her favorite dishes only.
* Wipes her side of the table first when a drink is spilled on both sides.
* Spends a long time on putting on her makeup.
* Is an attention seeker.
* Is self-righteous.
* Acts in a selfish manner.
* Uses offensive language.
* Is distrustful of men.
* Is self-centered.

Women with low estrogen levels tend to have many of the above qualities. Such women are likely to have negative effects on men.

ACUTE INTUITION OF WOMEN

A hormone called prolactin promotes secretion and stimulates maternal instincts. Prolactin levels increase dramatically during pregnancy and nearly double immediately before menstruation. When prolactin levels rise, the number of nerve cells in the olfactory sphere that stores olfactory-related memory increases. Consequently, certain smells may conjure up past memories. This keen sense of smell forms the basis of women's acute intuition.

HOW TO INVIGORATE AN ILL-FATED PERSON

Those who often encounter unfortunate events have a tendency to experience the intense effects of displeasure, leading to the buildup of stress in the brain. This, their predisposition is associated with the workings of the brain. To relieve stress, a hormone called TRH, which has motivating effects, should be fully utilized. To activate TRH, consciously try to do the following: do not blame others, do not complain, think positively, write down only pleasant experiences in a journal, and find pleasure in small matters.

BOOK NINE

STRATEGY OF MU

STRATEGY OF NOTHINGNESS

The strategy of nothingness is a way to have a sense of self by seeking a single source in principle of nature. The way means enlightenment. Enlightenment can be achieved by being honest with yourself. Enlightenment can be achieved by training. You need training in order to become closer to your natural self. And your natural self means your true self. Your true self can be found by making things simpler. When you can explain things in an easily understood manner, you become a real thing. You can make things simpler by throwing away what you already have rather than obtaining new things. This way, you get a liberating feeling. Abandon your ego and consign yourself to God. To achieve it, do everything within your power.

Mu-No-Heiho

Shingan (Mind's Eye) and *Ki* (Judgment and Will)

Satori (enlightenment) refers to a state of knowing, realizing and sensing. *Satori* in martial arts refers to a world where one's bodily function is in a good state and one can bring up its skill devotedly by controlling its mind and will.

Satori is achieved when one's mind connects to the mind of the universe. When one's mind connects to the mind of the universe, one comes to be able to understand reason of nature without being taught. When one's mind connects to the mind of the universe, one comes to bear supernatural power. Buddha described the supernatural world as *ku* (knowing the void).

The world of *ku*: While you are in meditation, there is a space and moment of *sei* (quietness), in which you don't hear any sound. In the moment of *sei*, there is only reverberation of sound. At the moment, you are standing at the gateway to *ku*, where the power of mighty nature exists.

In *ku*, there is energy that can draw out unlimited power. To draw out the power, first of all, you must start to simplify things. You must know the function of your mind through, and change the impure wave of your mind to a pure wave. The training refers to harmonizing *chi* (knowledge), *I* (intention) and *jyou* (emotion), and the act of carrying it out.

THE WISDOM OF *SHINGAN*

To lead your mind to *shingan*, you need to close your eyes lightly and open your mind's eye, which is situated in the middle of the eyebrows. Then, focus your thoughts on the one point and begin meditation. When your eyes are closed, there is another eye and it is called *shingan*, the third eye.

The part in the middle of the eyebrows is related to the energy of seeing, knowing and understanding things. It is also a point of spiritual awakening. When the energy blossoms, clairvoyance will be acquired.

Fundamental Knowledge of Breathing and Mind

There is a close connection between breathing and mind. When breathing is disturbed, one's mind is disturbed. When mind is disturbed, one's breathing is disturbed.

Tanden kokyu, involving *shin* (mind), *ki*, and *ryoku* (power) fulfills one's mind. *Tanden* is located about three centimeters below the navel. It is a source of the vitality, which operates on sex organs and the immune system. When the energy of *tanden* weakens, one is quick to be wearied. One also loses interest in the other sex.

Abdominal breathing focused on *tanden* can fulfill *ki*. The foundation of a fight lies in breathing. *Tanden kokyu* is practiced just before one starts a fight. First, put internal pressure on the stomach. Breathe long first and cut the breath short at the end from the mouth, saying "ha-a, ha." When the breathing is ready, integrate your mind and elevate your concentration.

When you confront the opponent, switch to nose breathing. Watch the opponent's movement by the rule of wild animal's fight. Animals inhale deeply just before the fight, and they hold their breath during the fight. The moment you notice the change of attack, your body has to already be in movement.

Fundamental Knowledge of *Yuin*

Yuin is *keiryaku* (strategy). To draw the opponent in the truth that you wish for, conceal the truth inside and infer the opponent's movement. *Yuin* is to achieve one's aim through secret *keiryaku*.

When you set *yuin*, you need to use your mind vigilantly. *Yuin* is to gain a victory by leading the opponent to anticipate.

Seeing the Opponent's Reaction to *Keiryaku*

Do not fix your eyes on a part of the opponent. You need to see the opponent's motion without seeing. This is to prevent the opponent from reading your mind and to keep the opponent's every movement. This is to know that you cannot see a big tree if you focus your mind on a leaf. Once you seize a chance, you must keep it at all costs.

Mental Disease

Mental disease is to stick to a certain idea. Mental disease is to freeze on certain things or victory. The mind can work freely, if one has enough room to be able to hear the sound of wind and water. One can control one's mind by releasing it. When one removes the source of thoughts, one's mind starts to be free from all thoughts. Master the road of experts who remove thoughts by gaining other thoughts.

Worldly desires results from obsessions. Obsessions inhabit a frozen mind and make it lose clear sight. One can return to natural self and demonstrate real feelings by dissolving the frozen mind and using it freely as if it flows throughout one's body. Opponents cannot pierce a mind that works freely.

Humans are *ku*. You are *ku*. Technique is also *ku*. Karate of *ku* is to demonstrate the invincible technique without concerning oneself about *ku* or fixing one's mind on *ku*. Once you attain this state, there is no enemy any more. Both those who challenge you and those who don't will perish.

It is not a disease to challenge opponents with a belief that you will win by all means as long as you use the technique properly. Do your best, leave the consequences to God's will.

THE BASIS OF *KEHAI* (SIGN, INDICATION)

Kehai refers to murder in the air, spiritual power, and second sight.

Kehai is human's electromagnetism and electromagnetic wave.

Humans come to bear magnetism through exercise. The human body is made up of atoms. Atoms come to bear electricity through the fluctuation of electrons. Then, positive and negative appear. The electrification can be classified into five groups.

Contact Electrification occurs through the contact of different electrons.

Peeling Electrification happens when adhered substances are pulled part.

Pressure Electrification occurs when substances are pressured.

Induction Electrification refers to the production of electricity in one object by another that already has electricity.

Friction Electrification occurs when substances are rubbed against each other.

Humans repeat cycles of electrifying and discharging constantly. A human's electrification system can hold a high voltage of 500 by combining these five effects. There is a difference among individuals in sensing the change of voltage because the human body functions as an antenna.

The electromagnetic wave that the human body emits is said to travel as far as 20 meters at the maximum. Partition by a wall does not affect the distance that the wave travels. Humans have the ability to sense the voltage as *kehai*.

Kehai lies in the body hair. The antenna responds to stimuli through the body hair. There is a difference among individuals in reaction, depending on the length and density of body hair. The hairier the person is, the more keened his sense is. The more static electricity is around, the more one's sense becomes blunted.

When you enter a room, you sometimes sense the *kehai* of the person who was in the room before you. The voltage of *kehai* is about 1800. It is the remaining electricity of the person who was there. The residual of humans' *kehai* remains for about ten minutes. You sense it as *kehai*.

Transformation of *Ki*

Ki lies in the source of life and fight.

* When one is angry, *ki* goes up. In serious cases, one occasionally vomits blood.
* When one is happy, *ki* settles down. When one is sad, *ki* fades out.
* When one is afraid, *ki* goes down and the abdomen becomes swollen.
* When it is cold, *ki* draws back and the defense of one's body weakens. When it is hot, *ki* slips out of one's body along with sweat.
* When one is surprised, *ki* is disturbed, the mind pounds wildly and the spirit floats. When discretion goes too far, *ki* is concentrated and the flow of *ki* goes up.
* Strain drains *ki* away. Strains cause one to sweat and snort.
* The five internal organs are full of *ki*. When the *ki* of the five organs runs out, one will be dead.
* When one's spirit is stimulated the energy falls down. The negativity runs short and one cannot generate new *ki*.

THE ORIGIN OF MARTIAL ARTS AND THE PRINCIPLE OF *RINNE* (THE WHEEL OF LIFE)

When the harmony of the universe and the harmony of the mind connect, one demonstrates superhuman power. When the power and technique are in harmony, they are on the wave of senses.

When everything including God, the great universe, enemies, and oneself become one, both the technique and mind ripen and reach the utmost of maturity.

When you attain the state of *uchusokuga*, you become aware of the origin or martial arts.

If there is hesitation in mind or a warp in strength and weakness, techniques cannot conform to the rhythm. The aim of martial arts is to gain the top of *ku*.

Uchusokuga

The Principal of *Rinne* (The Wheel of Life)

The origin of martial arts lies in *ku*.

Ku is God's will.

The will is *ku*.

Ku is the universe.

The universe is the law of nature.

The law of nature is the feeling of appreciation.

The feeling of appreciation is found in conducts.

The mind of conducts lies in the mind of reward.

The mind of reward lies in the mind of happiness.

The mind of happiness is the mind of love.

The mind of love is the mind of affection.

The mind of affection lies in the mind that is being kept alive.

The mind that is being kept live lies in the mind of mighty nature.

The mind of mighty nature lies in the mind of the sun.

The mind of the sun is the mind of the universe.

The mind of the universe lies in the egoless mind.

The egoless mind is the peaceful mind.

The peaceful mind lives in the harmonious mind.

The harmonious mind lies in the mind in which the mind, technique, and body are one.

The mind in which the mind, technique, and body are one is in the mind of martial arts.

The mind of martial arts is in the mind of *cyudou* (the golden mean).

The mind of *cyudou* lies in the mind of lies in the mind of *hassyoudou*.

Hassyoudou is right perspective, right thought, right action, right living, right effort, right contemplation, right understanding.

The mind of *hassyoudou* is in the mid of *houtou* (God's light, mind, and laws).

The mind of *houtou* is the mind of God.

The mind of God is the light of *shinri* (God's truth).

The light of *shinri* is in *ku*.

Ku lies in the origin of martial arts.

The origin of martial arts is *ku*.

Everything comes up to the principal of *rinne*.

Three Important Elements for Healthy Life

Three important elements for healthy life are mental health, exercise, and food. To meet and maintain these essential elements keeps you healthy.

Mental Health

Humans prefer being alone. We are not made to live in a group. Therefore, when many people gather in a small area, we end up getting stressed out. Try to be mentally stabilized and free from stress. When you pay attention to your mental health, it reflects on your physical health. You become mentally secure, and stress goes away.

Exercise

Move your body until you feel tired. Don't be afraid to be exhausted. It is perfect if you do exercises until your body gets wasted and regain power after one or two nights sleep. After you recover, you will find yourself reaching the next level because you went beyond your limit. Good training is to repeat tiredness efficiently.

Food

Choose the right foods and have healthy meals with balanced nutrition.

CHAPTER 2

Michi and *Ku* (Path and Emptiness)

All things originate from *ku*.

It's difficult to reach a state of *ku* only with scholastic knowledge.

A vast treasure trove of wisdom is hidden between lines of text and words.

That is where ku exists.

It has been conveyed that one who opens the door to the treasure trove can single-handedly experience the world of *ku*.

The Buddha has been cited as the first and only one to reach and preach the world of *ku*.

Michi　　　　　　　　　　Ku

SHINMYORYOKU (MIRACULOUS POWER)

In the world of *ku*, there exists invisible and incomprehensible infinite energy and wisdom. The energy called *shinmyoryoku* is hidden.

Shin is *mu*, which means "nothingness." *Mu* is a state in which one expresses *ku* (emptiness) on a conscious level. One does not have any obsession which allows free spiritual movement.

Myou means miraculous power or sense of spiritual presence.

Ryoku means of infinite movement.

In order to gain the mental and physical sensitivity of *shinmyoryoku*, one must purify his or her mind by eliminating fear and obsession. As a result, one will gain power in technique without obsession. The adversary's intention and movements will also be mirrored in one's mind which reacts and exerts infinite power filled with the miraculous power of *mu*.

Movements of an adversary become slow in one's eyes.

Shinri and *Michi* (Truth and Path)

Shinri (truth) shows the *michi* (path) of human life.

The one who practices truth should not lose his or her mind. One who learns only the technique will grow arrogant as his or her technique progresses.

An arrogant person will become degenerated and lack human nature.

By indulging in a sense of superiority, the body and technique will gradually decline.

The natural world is *mujyou* (transience).

A beautifully blossomed flower will eventually fall. This is fate.

The human body shares the same fate of growing old and death.

Therefore our mission is to train to develop one's mind and soul which will last forever in this world.

The one who searches for truth will be approached by evil.

Evil will lead one's mind into temptation and confusion, further away from the truth.

We live in a world of domestic confusion and social conflict which provides us a place for training. The training process could cause a lugubrious personality, a nervous breakdown, and temptation of sensual and material desire. Vanity will take our mind away.

A person who believes life is a one-time event will be ruled by avarice.

The one who falls for it will ruin one's life and get lost spiritually.

People control themselves with virtue. One must practice virtue to alleviate spiritual strains and remember peace of mind to appreciate the generosity of the gods.

Pursuit of Truth

In order to pursue truth, one must balance scholastic knowledge, custom, and a social environment and turn them into awareness training.

To practice awareness training, one must be affectionate and compassionate, believe in oneself and be spiritually comfortable to pursue truth.

Once a person begins to pursue truth, one will become spiritually focused and unified thereby revealing light in one's mind. The door to the vast treasure trove of wisdom opens to the world of *ku*.

Michi (Path)

Dou never answers in words. It makes you realize the existence of internal wisdom of the mind. It shows you the way of life. It teaches that the way you are is the truth.

People are swayed by worldly desire and obsessions. You don't have to worry. While you have a life, you do the best you can. When you die, you simply need to die.

Do not mistake the gate for the house (the truth) that stands inside.

Do not forget that you are on a parallel with the training to enable the low-layer fourth-dimensional *sii*, which draws negative power.

The most important thing is to use the mind of *choudou* as a monitor and carry out your goal of attaining *satori* of higher levels.

The internal fight is to try to control your fate by learning to control your spirit and feelings during a fight and facing the result of your decision and choice.

Deeds in Life

A daily deed starts and ends with appreciation.

In order to practice spiritual training to live like a decent human being, one should follow *cyu-do* (moderation) to live in harmony and to love.

One should keep all-encompassing love in mind with might.

Make a clear distinction between work, time off, and pleasure in order to live one's life like oneself.

In life, one should not lose standards, cooperation, equality, courage, appreciation, service, compassion, or love.

If they are lost, the individual, family, and society will collapse.

PRINCIPLES

Forerunners have discovered and confirmed principles through repeating experiences of trial and error. However, too much obsession with principles leads to incorrect conclusions.

Application of principle must always be flexible.

All principles of *hei-ho* apply to work.

It is unnecessary to be too concerned with different sects of schools such as karate.

One should absorb good things.

Fortune Telling, Spells

The theory of *hei-ho* requires giving up fortune telling and spells. *Hei-ho* is like *kido* (manipulation).

Onyou (the way of *yin* and *yang*) and fortune telling are effective ways to manage a fool.

No matter what one does, one should not be influenced by fortune telling and spells.

To achieve great results in battle, one should do all that is humanly possible.

Keep Moderation in Mind

When one's mind is boiling, pour on some cold water.
When one's mind is cold, pour on some hot water.
When one maintains cyudo (moderation), the mind will subside.

LEADER

Teaching is learning. Learning is personal growth.
Peace of mind is the result of personal growth.

By conveying peace of mind to others, leaders will move toward the correct direction. Teaching does not lead one to become a saint but make oneself worthy.

It is difficult to defeat oneself.

Without victory over oneself, it is difficult to teach michi (path) to others.

A leader's role is to provide serenity, responsibility, deeds and welfare.
Teaching requires a higher aspiration to lead others.
A leader should not be caught up in a single principle or opinion.
An unprejudiced and free mind will lead to truth.
One must be patient to guide others.
One must be flexible and have deep compassion.
One must not be rough with others but teach everyone equally.

Teaching Methods
Maternal Teaching Method—Respect others as mothers do. Do not fight.
Teach calmly.

Paternal Teaching Method—Be strict with others as fathers do. Do not
allow wrongdoing. Teach with discipline.

No matter which method one chooses, students will take after their
master.

It is very rare that students take after their master's good quality. Bad
qualities of the master are more likely to be handed down.

A master who hands bad qualities down to students often does not have
insight into their individual characteristics.

A master who cannot bring out the best from followers is not competent
to be a teacher.

A true master brings individual characteristics from students.

The master will guide students to express themselves in forms.

The one who can practice this is a qualified teacher.

A master's expression will come out through students in their posture
and form.

To become a teacher, one must have a tremendous amount of knowledge and wisdom to make others understand. On top of that, obtaining
stability is a minimum condition.

A master should intuitively know student's progress in comprehension
and techniques through their behavior, the color of their eyes, and slight
changes in facial expression. Changes of mind will appear in facial expressions as well as behavior. The teacher who has sensed it has the power to
see through to the student's potency.

Fellow Students

Good fellow students see one's strong points correctly.

They will be there to prevent you from making false conducts by guiding you to firm decision and judgment.

When one seeks to make a good friend with a fellow student, it is better to choose someone who encourages you to be courageous, is virtuous, and provides a positive influence.

A fellow student who can give and receive peace of mind and positive energy will enrich your life.

What Desire Means

There are different kinds of desire. There are morally right and wrong desires.

One might wish to work hard to make a lot of money and save it to contribute it to society. One might practice very hard to become famous and powerful and then use them to contribute to others.

Desire is a way for personal growth. However, too much wrong desire will be poisonous.

LIKE IS CURED BY LIKE

A master should be competent enough to take both good and evil.

A master should not choose someone for their good or evil but must have the ability to bring the best from someone's weakness.

Poison also has the power to cure.

A master should be able to become a poison to the adversary to save him or her.

In order to assimilate with poison, one must have wisdom and mercy.

BOOK TEN

THE PINNACLE OF
SPIRITUAL ATTAINMENT

STRATEGY OF NOTHINGNESS

A path will be revealed only when you read a sutra with a warm heart and put its teachings into practice. Otherwise, a sutra has no value in life. It is no exaggeration to say that it will take more than a lifetime for a reader to carry out every recommendation in a book.

Without action, peace cannot be maintained at home or a country cannot be governed. There is a limit to how much one can learn from literature. On the contrary, if you learn by utilizing the power of the mind, the amount of knowledge you can acquire will be unlimited. Once you are determined to reach a goal on your own, you will feel a sense of calmness. With such determination, you will never depend on anyone or act cowardly or contemptibly toward others. Since you have nothing to be envious of, your mind will be pure.

Narrow mindedness prevents one from seeing the truth. Your mind must be wide open. Observing reality from one's standpoint will only reveal half the truth because one's ego obstructs the view. The self must be discarded to be able to see the true nature of reality. Discarding the self requires skill.

Without leaving this shore, the opposite shore can never be reached. This shore symbolizes the world of *shiki* (form), or the realm of the naked eye, whereas the other shore symbolizes the world of *ku* (emptiness), or the realm of the mind's eye.

Shin-Gyo

In the Heart Sutra, *shiki* represents a world that is perceived by the naked eye, while *ku* represents a world that is perceived by the mind's eye. The body is *shiki*; the mind and the soul are *ku*. The principal character in the Heart Sutra is *Kan-jizai-bosatsu* (the Bodhisattva Avalokitesvara). *Kan-jizai-bosastsu* is a truth seeker who is on the threshold of realizing *ku*, which is the final stage of enlightenment. Through self-cultivation, he has acquired the ability to perceive the past, present, and future. *Kan-jizai-bosastsu*, or Avalokitesvara in the original language, symbolizes the Buddha's enlightenment. The Heart Sutra is essentially a dialogue, in which *Kan-jizai-bosatsu* speaks to Sariputra. Sariputra is one of the ten leading disciples of the Buddha and is considered the wisest of all. In the Heart Sutra, negative thoughts are repeated to produce a positive meaning. In *ku* there is absolutely nothing that can be seen by the naked eye; however, there are things that can be seen by the mind's eye.

The notion of *ku* is fundamental to Buddhist philosophy. In the Heart Sutra, *ku* is expressed in the phrases "*Shiki soku ze ku*" and "*Ku soku ze shiki.*" In *ku*, two opposing aspects such as negation and affirmation, or non-existence and existence, are unified and integrated. Any attempt to comprehend the concept of *ku* must begin with understanding the notion of *innen* (paticca-samuppada or dependent origination). *Ku* and *innen* are two sides of the same coin. Being enlightened means to clearly understand the doctrine of dependent origination. Only a handful of those ubiquitous seekers of truth actually arrive at truth. Truth is found by those who are earnestly devoted to their search for truth.

The Pinnacle of Spiritual Attainment – The Heart Sutra

The original source of the concept of *ku* (emptiness).

To fully comprehend East Asian Cultures, the world of the Heart Sutra must be understood. The Heart Sutra elucidates the notion of *ku*. This sutra is the origin of Buddhism as well as the martial arts and other forms of art. *Ku* is the ultimate source of everything. In your search for enlightenment, you must focus on understanding the meaning of *ku* as it is equivalent to comprehending all the central tenets of Buddhism. Bookish knowledge alone cannot guide you to enlightenment. The realm of *ku* can only be reached by those who can uncover the goldmine of wisdom hidden beneath written words. Infinite energy and wisdom, invisible to the naked eye, are present in the world of *ku*. It is a place where supernatural *waza* (technique) called *shin-mo-ryoku* (miracle power) is possible. To develop *shin-mo-ryoku*, one needs to purify his mind, remove fears, abandon attachment, and sharpen his mind and body. By doing so, spontaneity will be added to one's skill, allowing one to manipulate the opponent's mind as he pleases. This is how one can fully utilize *shin-mo-ryoku*.

How did the Buddha reach a state of *ku*? How did truth seekers of later generations attempt to make their way into the realm the Buddha had entered? What is the truth of the universe? What is the meaning of life? What are the purpose and duty of being alive in this world? How many of us know the answers to these questions?

Truth reveals the right path to us. Those in pursuit of truth should not lose sight of the right path. A person who learns techniques without following the right path will grow conceited as skill improves. A conceited person will become corrupt, eventually losing humane qualities. The natural world has no mercy. You may temporarily feel superior to other people, but in the meantime, your body and skill are gradually deteriorating. Beautiful flowers, blooming all their glory, are destined to wither and fall before long. Humans cannot escape from their destiny. The physical body is bound to grow old and die. It is our fate to encounter unpleasant people and to be separated from those we love. Our duty in this world is to engage in spiritual practice to polish our everlasting mind and soul. Eventually, we will all vanish from this world.

Some people become obsessed with sexual and materialistic desires and greed for money, believing that they have only this life to live. Such people have gone morally astray. By following the right path, you can control yourself and straighten the distorted ideas in your mind. When your mind is at peace, you will naturally appreciate God's generosity. The purpose of the martial arts is not to create confusion; rather, practitioners of the martial arts attain inner tranquility by being grateful and saying "thank you" loudly in their mind. How should we go about pursuing truth? First, we must create a social environment conducive to learning a wide range of subjects and forming good habits. In such an environment, the way we train our mind will inevitably change. While searching for truth, you must always maintain inner peace, so that you can have confidence in yourself and act affectionately and compassionately toward others. Moreover, you must also learn to focus your mind. Then a ray of light will penetrate your heart, uncovering a treasure house of wisdom containing the secrets of *ku*.

We have a natural tendency to be swayed by our desire and attachment. There is no reason to brood over this tendency. We should live our life to the fullest while we are alive; the time will soon come when we all have to die. Enlightenment is achieved when your mind and the mind of the universe are united. This union gives you a supernatural power. The Buddha called this state of mind *ku*. What happens in the realm of *ku*? While practicing meditation, you may temporarily lose the sense of hearing. Then, there comes a point where all sounds disappear with only reverberations left behind. At that moment, when everything becomes silent, you are standing at an entrance to the world of *ku*, where the energy of Mother Nature resides.

In my childhood, I experienced detachment of my soul from the body while I was suffering from a high fever. To my surprise, my separate self was looking down at my body from above. This mystic experience impelled me to explore the unknown realms. After experimenting with various forms of the martial arts, I finally stepped into the field of *karate-do*, where no weapons are allowed. Out in the real world, my life has been dictated by worldly successes and failures, like a small boat rocking on the big waves. These experiences have raised many questions in my mind: What is the physical body? What is the relationship between the mind and body? How can we derive peace of mind when we are consumed with uncertainty and anxiety? What is happiness? What are the right attitudes toward life? What skills are required in *hei-ho* (art of warfare)?

This book attempts to unravel the mysteries of *waza* (technique) and the mind based on my past experience as well as what I have learned and inherited from our forerunners. It is not easy to maser the secrets of the martial arts. However, such secrets will be slowly revealed as your eyes gradually open through continual physical training. We are naturally endowed with the ability to act with complete freedom. This ability will shine brilliantly if polished constantly.

Yuu-ki

Introduction to the Heart Sutra

The World of the Heart Sutra

The Heart Sutra explains the essence of enlightenment, which was taught orally by the Buddha to his disciples. *Ku* is the pinnacle of spiritual awakening as well as the ultimate source of everything. *Ku* exists in an invisible realm. The Buddha was the first and only person to describe the invisible world. It is believed that the crux of "the Maha-prajna-paramita Sutra (Great Wisdom Sutra)," consisting of 600 volumes, is summarized in the Heart Sutra. Its essence is encapsulated in this short sutra, composed of a title (10 letters) and a text (266 letters). The Heart Sutra has been called "the scripture of wisdom." It provides a profound view of life and the universe. We can look to this sutra for guidance on how to live and what to study. The Heart Sutra has also been used as an incantation. Believers chant this sutra to protect themselves from evil spirits and disease. When in despair, transcribing this sutra helps believers to break free from suffering and eliminate attachment. The aim of the Heart Sutra is to liberate the mind.

The Buddha's Life: Becoming a Truth Seeker and Attaining Enlightenment

The Buddha was born in 463 BCE as a prince of a province called Mattodanarashinyan in Kapilavastu. He was born in Lumbini, what is now southern Nepal. His family belonged to the Sakya clan. At the time of his birth, India was mired in warfare and the people were suffering great hardship and starvation. Furthermore, the common people were being subjected to oppression under the caste system. One day, the Buddha stepped out of his palace and encountered a funeral. This experience prompted him to reflect deeply on the issue of life and death. At the age of 29, he left his wife and child and relinquished the headship of the family to embark on a spiritual journey. After six years of ascetic training, he realized that a harmonious,

118 BOOK TEN: THE PINNACLE OF SPIRITUAL ATTAINMENT

peaceful state of mind could be achieved by practicing the middle path. He was 35 years old at the time. What became clear to him was that purification of the mind eventually lead to tranquility of the mind. The Buddha taught that one's social position, reputation, and economic status in this world are totally meaningless in the context of enlightenment.

The Origin of the Heart Sutra

Ninety days after the Buddha's death, Mahaakassapa, Ananda, and Upali, the leading disciples of the Buddha, summoned 475 fellow disciples to a cave near Venuuvana-vihaara in Magadha to preserve his teachings. The disciples confirmed the Buddha's teachings in an effort to transmit them orally to future generations. This group's efforts provided a basis for the "Maha-prajna-paramita Sutra (Great Wisdom Sutra)," the essence of which is captured by the Heart Sutra (Hannya Shingyo). The text discussed in this book was translated by Genzo Sanzo (602-664 CE). This version is written in Chinese characters, which are used as phonetic symbols to represent Sanskrit words in the original text. Therefore, paying too much attention to these characters may obscure the true meaning of the text. The Heart Sutra describes a world that cannot be comprehended with academic knowledge. It is a world that can only be understood with empirical knowledge.

Genzo Sanzo was originally from Changan in the Tang Dynasty. Having studied Buddhism in India for 19 years, he returned to China to propagate Buddhist scriptures. The Heart Sutra was introduced to Japan in 609. The oldest Sanskrit palm-leaf text in the world (called "*Horyuji-basho-bonhon*") exists in Japan. This text is 40 years older than the one translated by Genzo. The Heart Sutra widely available today in Southeast Asia and Japan is the version translated by Genzo.

It was Bodhidharma, founder of Shorinji, who integrated the elements of *zazen*, the martial arts, and the Heart Sutra. He emphasized the importance of *zazen* practice as a means of understanding the realm of the mind that defied verbal expression. By the time Eno (638-713), sixth master of Shorinji, came along, a method of Zen practice had been devised, in which the practitioners attempted to explore the realm of the mind by studying the notion of *ku* expounded in the Heart Sutra. The development of Zen Buddhism nearly coincides with the period during which Genzo made significant contributions to Buddhism.

The Revolution in Buddhism

Buddhism can be roughly divided into the Hinayana and Mahayana schools. Hinayana Buddhism has been called ancient Buddhism that emphasizes the original teachings of the Buddha. Hinayana Buddhism is intended for experts of Buddhism and those who lead a monastic life to attain enlightenment. In the Hinayana tradition, only a handful of monks can achieve enlightenment. Ordinary people admire the monks and try to derive some benefit from their achievements. Hinayana Buddhism is meant for specialists rather than for laypeople. Hinayana denotes a small vehicle (which means that enlightenment is attained through self-endeavor).

Mahayana Buddhism came into existence as a revolutionary movement against Hinayana Buddhism. Mahayana Buddhism holds that everyone is capable of attaining enlightenment. Followers of the Mahayana tradition, also called "*Zaike* (laypeople) Buddhism," can practice their religion without renouncing their home or work. An ideal practitioner of Mayahana Buddhism is an individual who attains perfect enlightenment by finding salvation for himself as well as for others. Mahayana denotes a large vehicle, indicating that all travelers can become enlightened together. Mahayana literature explains the notion of *ku* most succinctly.

Meditation and Fasting

Buddhist training includes meditation and fasting. The objective of meditation and fasting is to cultivate the power, wisdom, and potential ability of the brain. It is believed that meditation and fasting can activate the unused portions of the brain, thereby unlocking their potential. When mental activity is suspended, people stop responding to changes in their surroundings; as a result, the immeasureable energy that exists within you will be unleashed. We tend to treat the human mind, brain, intellect, intuition, body, and soul as independent beings; however, in reality, they are all interconnected. Meditation and fasting provide a means of repairing the circuits that have been broken by low vibration frequencies and imbalance. Becoming obsessed with meditation and fasting can cause illness, keep you away from enlightenment. The Buddha preached the importance of following the middle path. Enlightenment is a state of *ku* and *mu* where the mind is free from any attachment. Being enlightened means to triumph with perfect composure under and circumstances.

Training and Consciousness in the Martial Arts

Training for the martial arts must be done repeatedly.

Repeated exercised can alter the level of our consciousness. Once the level of your consciousness is lowered through your continual training without sleep, your mind will be kept awake. Meditation and *zazen*, by dropping the level of your consciousness, can intensify the power of *ki* (life force) without sacrificing your concentration or observational ability. By performing strenuous exercises over and over again, your skill will improve to the point where you are no longer preoccupied with your skill or mind. This is how you alter the level of your consciousness. *Karate-do* is called *do-zen* (an active form of Zen) because of its training methods, in which practitioners practice *waza* persistently until the level of their consciousness is brought down. Through rigorous training, you can renounce desire and attain inner peace.

The Buddha's Meditation and *Bo-No* (Distracting Thoughts)

The Buddha's spiritual journey began with an attempt to extinguish eight types of *bon-no*: desire, hatred, hunger and thirst, delusion, drowsiness, fear, doubt, and obstinacy. *Bon-no* is something that hinders you from attaining enlightenment. It is a rebellious force that arises from the mind. It is a challenge to eliminate *bon-no* that springs from our instincts. The Buddha took up this challenge by meditating and performing *zazen*. The first *bon-no* was desire and he eliminated it by rectifying his mind. The second rebellious force was hatred. Next came hunger and thirst, delusion, drowsiness, fear, doubt, and finally, obstinacy. Each of these rebellious forces, representing the eight kinds of *bon-no*, originated in his mind. The Buddha succeeded in fending off the rebel forces without being attached to them, thereby finding a prescription and a method for defeating such forces. He had discovered the doctrine of dependent origination, which holds that one's fate is determined by cause and effect, and the Four Noble Truths, which explain the cause of suffering (the Eightfold Path shows how such suffering can be terminated). Satan harassed the Buddha for seven years, trying to tempt him into abandoning his search for truth, but failed to penetrate the Buddha's mind. The Buddha overcame temptation placed in his way by Satan's forces and finally realized enlightenment under the bodhi tree.

Bo-no

What is Nirvana?

The Buddha's main objective was to rise above suffering. For the Buddha, nirvana represented an ideal place, where one lives in absolute tranquility and peace completely liberated from suffering. There are two types of nirvana:

Incomplete Nirvana.

All distracting thoughts have been extinguished, but you are still alive and are trapped in the physical body. You can still feel physical pain. Buddha attained this nirvana under the bodhi tree at the age of 35.

Complete Nirvana

Your physical body has perished after death. Buddha entered this nirvana when he died in Kusinagara at the age of 80.

Hannya (Prajna)

The term *hannya* signifies wisdom that guides us to enlightenment. *Hannya* denotes intuitive sagacity that enables us to look at the true nature of existence. It represents genuine wisdom with profound rationality. This intuitive wisdom is attained when desire is completely extinguished. *Hannya Shingyo* has been recited mostly as an incantation rather than as a sutra. The power and magic of this sutra continue to fascinate people. This sutra is said to have a mystical power; one can find salvation by chanting it and attain happiness by being conscious of it. The notion of *ku* in *Hannya Shingyo* is one of the key concepts in Buddhist philosophy.

Ku and *Mu*

Zen Buddhism emphasizes the concept of *Mu*, which symbolizes enlightenment. *Mu* is absolute nothingness that transcends the conflict between existence and non-existence. This notion defies comparisons with other concepts. *Mu* is existence itself. In Zen Buddhism, becoming *mu* means to grasp the ultimate nature of reality, which allows you to achieve enlightenment. *Mu* does not signify a blank state of mind; rather, *mu* represents detachment from the five organs of the body after understanding their functions. The concept of *ku*, on the other hand, may evoke the image of a void.

However, *ku* is a positive notion in Buddhism and the martial arts. The concept of *ku*, with its limited potential, can transform itself flexibly depending on how one interprets it. Once you gain a clear insight into the empty nature of existence, you can reach a state of *ku* where neither attachment nor suffering exists. Ku itself represents enlightenment; *kara* in the term *karate-do* signifies this ideal state.

Zen and Hannya Shingyo

Zen Buddhism has stressed the importance of instruction through psychological interactions rather than theoretical discussions. Whereas translators in the past treated Hannya Shingyo as a scripture that captured the essence of the Maha-prajna-paramita Sutra (Great Wisdom Sutra), the phrases "*Shi-ki-soku-ze-ku*" and "*Ku-soku-ze-shiki*," both of which explain the meaning of *ku*, have been considered important. Zen Buddhism, in contrast, has emphasized the phrase, "*Shin-mu-gei-ge.*" This sutra is invaluable for Zen Buddhists because it illustrates how abandonment of attachment to delusional reality can lead to enlightenment. This means that Zen Buddhism has taken a new approach, in which Hannya Shingyo is construed as a practical text rather than a theoretical one. In this approach, Hannya Shingyo, the martial arts, and other art forms are all linked together, thereby realizing a state of *mu*.

To pursue enlightenment is to search for immeasurable truth, to acquire the ability manipulate life at will, to investigate phenomena that originate in our mind, and to undergo training to recall what our ancestors and predecessors had learned. The aim of the martial arts is not only to unveil the true nature and the laws of the universe through mental and physical exercises, but also to attain eternal tranquility. Enlightenment is achieved when the mind and body are guided to a higher dimension. An enlightened person holds no attachment to his skill or mind, let alone other worldly matters. This means that such a person knows how to practice the middle path.

Hannya Shingyo

The Martial Arts and Truth

The martial arts offer a path you can follow to unravel the mysteries of life and the soul. The ultimate goal is to reach a state of *ku* and *mu*. The purpose of the martial arts as well as religion is to connect the divine will (God) and the mind (human being).

Mu symbolizes freedom of mind without any attachment. In the martial arts, *mu* represents a world where superhuman *waza* called *shin-myo-ryoku* is possible. *Shin-myo-ryoku* can be acquired only when the mind's eye is open. Past sages and masters equated opening of the mind's eye with enlightenment. These sages and masters, with a propensity to be audacious, challenged common sense and scientific knowledge of the day. Their boldness provoked ridicule and rejection by people, making their own lives difficult. This happened because these sages and masters had a desire to impose their beliefs on others. To suppress this urge, they practiced meditation and reflected deeply on their conduct.

The aim of meditation lies in introspection. Meditation without self-examination is useless because distortion of the mind is not corrected. As a result, you may easily succumb to temptation or your mind may not function properly. Your preoccupation with attachment makes you vulnerable to temptation. Consequently, attachment grows even stronger, preventing you from engaging in introspection. This may lead to mental illness such as schizophrenia or physical disorders. As self-examination progresses, your mind will be liberated, allowing you to perceive changes in the environment clearly without any effort. The ability to observe the past, present, and future may also gradually develop.

Meditation should be practiced at night, when silence reigns. The ideal time for meditation is when the magnetic field is most stable. The magnetic field stabilizes around the time of the solar or lunar eclipse. You can restore the balance of your mind and body through meditation. First, close your eyes lightly and try to see straight through the middle of your forehead. Focus your attention on the third eye located in the middle of the forehead. You may become drowsy when your eyes are closed. However, you can shake off drowsiness and stay awake by opening the mind's eye and looking straight ahead. While meditating, try to breathe in harmony with other living creatures in nature.

According to Buddha, we are born into this world to discover the true nature of our existence. The world we live in is constrained by the energy of consciousness. After going through various experiences and finding fulfillment in this world, we travel to the realm of *ku*. We will discover the ultimate source of the self in *ku* after experiencing transmigration. Then a new life will be born, which will repeat the cycle of reincarnation.

The Essence of the Heart Sutra

The Heart Sutra is an expression of the mind of the Buddha. After attaining enlightenment, the Buddha preached *shi-tai* (suffering, cause, extinction, path) and the doctrine of dependent origination (paticca-samuppada) for 45 years. East Asian cultures including Japanese culture cannot be comprehended unless you understand these teachings of Buddha.

Three Ways to Practice Buddhism

Sei-mon-jo or sravaka-yana: Practitioners dutifully follow the teachings of the Buddha and the sutras by means of listening. This is a traditional Buddhist practice that belongs to Hinayana Buddhism. Practitioners live in a communal life in a monastery.

En-gaku-jo or Pratyekabuddha-yana: Practitioners lead a solitary life deep in the mountains. They attain enlightenment by observing changes of nature; for instance they may watch wildflowers burst into bloom and leaves fall off the trees. These practitioners become enlightened on their own. This method belongs to Hinayana Buddhism.

Bo-satsu-jo or Bodhisattva-yana: Practitioners seek enlightenment for themselves as well as for the benefit of others. There is no distinction between the self and others in this practice, which belongs to Mahayana Buddhism.

Each of these practices has its merits. Remember that their ultimate goal is the same: to realize enlightenment. The Heart Sutra is a scripture that belongs to the Mahayana school.

Understanding the Heart Sutra

If you have a desire to move a mountain closer to you, discard your desire and simply walk toward the mountain. To understand this logic, you need to understand the concept of *ku*. The Heart Sutra explains how you can move the mountain.

Once a monk posed a question: "Can you stop the movement of the boat over there?" In response, one monk closed his eyes. When one's eyes are closed, the mind is in a state of *ku*, where no boat exists. Another monk stood up and closed the shoji screen so that the boat could not be seen. This is also a state of *ku*, in which the movement of the board stops. Still another monk replied, "I wouldn't close my eyes or the shoji screen. I would become one with the boat, so that the boat should stop moving, at least in my mind." *Ku* has no distinction or attachment. Supreme freedom and *shin-myo-ryoku* exist in *ku*. *Ku* is enigmatic. *Ku* contains nothing. This is how ku is interpreted in Zen.

CHAPTER 2

The Buddha's Twelve Links of Dependent Origination

The Buddha underwent twelve stages of transformation as a human being from birth to death. He also experienced this chain of transformation in reverse order from death to *mu-myo* (ignorance).

1. *Mu-myo* – the self.
   Mu-myo is the origin of suffering. It is the root cause of all problems.

2. *Gyo* (action)
   A new life is conceived through sexual intercourse.

3. *Shiki* (consciousness)
   Consciousness emerges in the womb of a mother.

4. *Myo-shiki* (name and form)
   A body begins to form in the womb.

5. *Roku-Nyu* (development of the six sense organs.
   With the five body parts and six sense organs fully developed, the fetus is about to leave the womb.

6. *Soku* (contact)
   The newborn baby still cannot distinguish between warmness and coldness due to lack of the sense of touch.

7. *Ju* (sensation)
   By coming into contact with external objects, the senses start producing sensations.

8. *Ai* (love)
   Attachment to objects of one's desire develops.

9. *Shu* (grasping)
   A desire for possession arises.

10. *U* (becoming)
    A craving to possess everything in the world appears.

11. *Sei* (life)
    Sei makes human existence possible.

12. *Ro-shi* (old age and death)
    All life enfolds old age and death.

Note: The term "Buddha" means an enlightened being in Sanskrit. The real name of the Buddha, or *shaku-son*, was Gautama Siddhartha.

Mu-myo

CHAPTER 3

The Twelve Links of Dependent Origination

After gaining a deep insight into the nature of suffering, the Buddha found that it was the twelve links of dependent origination that gave rise to suffering.

1. *Mu-myo* – the ignorant self.
   Not knowing truth, one is disoriented. Ignorance of truth leads to suffering.

2. *Gyo* – habitual entanglement in trouble.
   Being unaware of truth, one is sowing the seeds of suffering by perpetrating bad deeds involving physical, verbal, and mental actions.

3. *Shiki* – consciousness.
   Roku-Shiki (sight, hearing, smell, taste, touch, and intellect), or six forms of consciousness, bring about suffering. According to Buddha, there are casual relationships among *nit-tai* (conception) and *shu-tai* (birth).

4. *Myo-shiki* – name and consciousness.
   Roku-kyo (form, voice, scent, flavor, contact, law) or objects of the six sense organs, creates suffering.

5. *Roku-sho*
   Roku-sho refers to *roku-kon*. *Kon* denotes sensation or perception. *Roku-kon* (eye, nose, ear, tongue, body, mind), or the sex sense organs, is the cause of suffering.

6. *Soku* – contact.
    Suffering emerges from the interplay of *roku-kon*, *roku-kyo*, and *roku-shiki*.

7. *Ju* – sensation.
    Sensations produced in the mind give rise to suffering.

8. *Ai* – love.
    Attachment to desire brings about suffering.

9. *Shu* – grasping.
    Yon-shu is the cause of suffering. *Yon-shu* including *yoku-sho*, *ken-shu* (drsti-paramarsa), *kaigon-shu* (sila-vrate-upadana), and *kago-shu* refers to different types of desire.

10. *U* – becoming.
    U refers to existence that arises from one's desire. *Ju* occasions *Shu*, which in turn occasions *U*. Whenever there is a cause, there will be an effect.

11. *Sho* – life.
    Life engenders desire for love. Life is permeated with hardships. Life is the cause of suffering.

12. *Ro-shi* – old age and death.
    It is painful to grow old and face death. Suffering always results from a cause. Reincarnation is inevitable.

Note: the Buddha, after acquiring a profound knowledge of the twelve *in-nen/engi* (the twelve links of dependent origination), discovered *shi-tai* (suffering, accumulation, extinction, path) and the Eightfold Path, which eventually led him to enlightenment.

Yon-tai (Shi-tai)

Hat-sho-do

CHAPTER 4

Shi-tai (The Four Noble Truths)

Shi-tai refers to four truths.

Ku (suffering): the self is the source of suffering.
Ju (accumulation): Suffering results when various causes of suffering accumulate. Suffering arises from attachment.
Metsu (extinction): By removing attachment, suffering is extinguished.
Do (path): the Eightfold Path. Practice of the middle path is recommended.

1. Right Perspective.
2. Right Thought.
3. Right Action.
4. Right Living.
5. Right Effort.
6. Right, Straightforward Effort.
7. Right Contemplation
8. Right Understanding

Chu-do

BOOK ELEVEN

THE HEART SUTRA

THE HEART SUTRA – A COMPLETE TRANSLATION

How to Contemplate and Act to Realize Prajnaparamita (Perfect Wisdom) That Innately Exists in our Mind.

Shiki Soku Ze Ku

Kan-jizai-bosatsu, an enlightened being with the ability to perceive various phenomena in the past, present, and future at will, practiced prajnaparamita (perfect wisdom) he had gained to observe the ultimate nature of existence. Then he discovered that the source of suffering was desire and attachment, which originated in five shandhas (body, sensation, expression, will, and knowledge).

Listen, Sariputra, all truths arising from *innen* (paticca-samuppada or dependent origination) are empty. *Shiki* (form) and *ku* (emptiness), and *ku* and *shiki* are not different, but the same. *Ju* (sensation), *so* (expression), *gyo* (will), and *shiki* (knowledge) are also the same. So are the mind and body. Sariputra, various physical phenomena are manifestations of truth. In *ku*, nothing is born or destroyed. The notion of filthiness or cleanness does not exist. There is no human concept of increasing or decreasing. To state it correctly, nothing in *Ku* can be seen by the naked eye. There is no sensation, expression, will, or knowledge. No eye, ear, nose, tongue, body, or mind. No *roku-kyo* (objects of the six sense organs), including form, voice, scent, flavor, contact, and law (truth). As I have said, *ku* contains nothing, neither the visible world nor the world detectable by consciousness. No limit or attachment exists in the world of *ku*. In *ku*, there is no illusion or dispelling of illusion. No old age or death; no termination of old age or death. No *shi-tai* (the Four Noble Truths), which consists of suffering, accumulation, extinction, or path. There is no truth in *ku*. No wisdom or attainment. Nothing is attained. No enlightenment or enlightened being. With nothing to be attained, attachment never arises. Bodhisattvas, or enlightened beings, are fearless because their minds are completely liberated. With distracting thoughts expelled from their minds and having attained every virtue, they are free from illusion, thereby realizing eternal peace of mind. Having transcended the past, present, and future, all buddhas are capable of acquiring supreme, right, and universal wisdom, owing to a thorough understanding of prajnaparamita (perfect wisdom). Prajnaparamita itself is a magnificent mantra, a sacred mantra with the power to conquer evil, a mantra that uncovers perfect wisdom. It is the supreme mantra, the unparalleled mantra, the true mantra without falsification that can eradicate all suffering. Therefore the mantra of prajnaparamita can be recited in the following way:

I have reached a state of *ku*. I have assisted others in attaining a state of *ku*. I have assisted everyone in achieving one's goal. Hence perfect enlightenment is attained. The Hannya Shingyo. The End.

Ha-ra-mit-ta

MAIN TEXT OF THE HEART SUTRA

1. *MA KA HAN NIYA HA RA MI TA SHIN GYO*

How to contemplate and act to realize perfect wisdom that innately exists in our mind.

2. *KAN ZI ZAI BO SATSU*

Kan-jizai-bosatsu is a savior of great insight and wisdom, who promotes enrichment of the mind in an effort to ease people's suffering. A pathfinder. A person who is on the threshold of realizing perfect enlightenment. Kan-jizai-bosatsu, or Avalo-kite-svara, symbolizes the Buddha's enlightenment. Having attained enlightenment, he is capable of perceiving all phenomena in the past, present, and future at will. However, at this stage, he has not completely detached himself from attachment. Kan-jizai-bosatsu is the embodiment of infinite compassion. He is willing to sacrifice himself to save people, without expecting anything in return. The Heart Sutra depicts a state of enlightenment reached by Kan-jizai-bosatsu. Kan-jizai denotes freedom of mind, which makes subjective and objective observation possible. The act of observing involves the naked eye as well as the mind's eye.

3. *GYO ZIN HAN NYA HA RA MIT TA ZI*

Kan-jizai-bosatsu became enlightened through daily practice that focused on the right path. The recognition of the empty nature of five skandhas or aggregates (body, sensation, expression, will, knowledge) relived him of all distress. He learned that eternal tranquility could be attained by maintaining the balance between the mind and body, practicing the middle path, and eliminating attachment. Having gained great insight and wisdom, Kan-jizai-bosatsu became a savior who strove to terminate people's suffering.

The two major components of the world are the mind and body, or spirit and substance. According to the Buddha, *shiki* (form) represents the body and substance, whereas *ku* (emptiness) represents the mind and spirit. The essence of the Heart Sutra is summarized in the notions of *ku* and *shiki*.

4. *SHO KEN GO ON KAI / KU DO IT SAI KU YAKU*

A careful observation reveals that five skandhas are all empty. This realization terminates all suffering. Kan-jizai-bosatsu, while practicing prajnaparamita in the real world, observed the true nature of existence and found that the origin of all suffering was desire and attachment, which sprang from five skandhas (body, sensation, expression, will and knowledge.)

To end suffering and obtain security of mind, the cause of suffering must be understood. Suffering will plague us ceaselessly, but there is a way to control our mind to minimize suffering and attain inner peace. All existence is empty. A deep insight into the concept of *ku* will lead us to a state of peace where suffering no longer exists. Once armed with the knowledge that five skandhas are all empty, we can break the bondage to suffering.

5. *SHA RI SHI*

Sariputra. (The Buddha is calling his name.) Originally a Brahmanist monk, Sariputra was one of the chief disciples of the Buddha, considered the wisest of all. He was born into a Brahmanist family in Magadha, which was situated in central India. One day, Sariputra encountered Assaji, a disciple of the Buddha. Assaji preached the doctrine of dependent origination, one of the core teachings of the Buddha, to Sariputra, saying that "everything arises from *en* (fate, destiny) and perishes according to *en*." Upon learning this principle, Sariputra abandoned Brahmanism to become the Buddha's disciple, along with his friend, MoKuren (Maudgalyaayana). Assaji, who taught the doctrine of dependent origination to Sariputra, was one of the five attendants of the Buddha, when he left his family in search for truth. Assaji practiced asceticism with the Buddha for six years. The Buddha, however, began to question the usefulness of self-mortification and eventually realized that ascetic practices could not bring about enlightenment. With this realization, he ate milk porridge offered by a woman named Sujata, to recover from fatigue. Witnessing this, the five attendants assumed that the Buddha had abandoned his quest for truth. Disappointed, they left him and went to a place called Mrgadava. After renouncing ascetic practices and regaining his strength, the Buddha finally attained enlightenment under the bodhi tree in Buddhagaya by engaging in deep meditation. Having discovered the law of dependant origination and the Four Noble Truths, he left the bodhi tree and followed the trail of his five attendants. After they were reunited, the Buddha delivered a sermon on enlightenment. Strongly moved by his sermon, the five attendants became the Buddha's first disciples. Assaji was one of them.

6. *SHIKI FU I KU / KU FU I SHIKI*

Form is not different from translation. Therefore, form is the same as emptiness.

Emptiness is not different from form. Therefore, emptiness is the same as form.

Since form and emptiness are one and the same, they are inseparable. *Shiki* represents the physical realm, substance and body, all of which can be seen by the naked eye.

Ku represents the existential realm, soul, and mind, none of which can be seen by the naked eye.

The world of *ku* can be perceived only when the mind's eye is open. When reduced to its simplest form, substance ultimately turns into particles, becoming invisible and empty. The five skandhas, including sensation, thought, will, knowledge, and consciousness, are equally empty. When *ku* takes on complex shapes, it manifests itself as physical objects. *Ku* is a world of eternity and infinity. The body and mind, or the mind and body, cannot be treated as independent entities since they are inseparable.

This line symbolizes the clash between the knowledge gained from academic study and prajnaparamita (perfect wisdom) acquired empirically through the process of samsara (reincarnation).

7. *SHIKI SOKU ZE KU / KU SOKU ZE SHIKI*

Shiki Soku Ze Ku – Form is the same as emptiness. The visible world of *shiki* constitutes the invisible world of *ku*. Likewise the body constitutes the mind. The visible world of *shiki* is a gateway to the invisible world of *ku*. The existence of a visible world necessitates the existence of an invisible world. All physical phenomena are devoid of substance. A physical object cannot retain its shape forever.

Ku Soku Ze Shiki – Emptiness is the same as form. Emptiness and form are identical. This phrase is opposed to "*Shiki Soku Ze Ku.*" The presence of an invisible world necessitates the presence of a visible world. The absence of substance necessitates the existence of physical phenomena. The mind constitutes the body.

The term emptiness may evoke the image of a void. However, the presence of *ki* (life force) in *ku* makes it possible for *shiki* to appear in the visible world. Permanence is not permanent and impermanence is not impermanent. This logic is explained in line seven.

This is the most famous line in the Heart Sutra. The character *kara*, or *ku*, in *karate-do* was taken from this line. The crux of the heart sutra is encapsulated in this single line.

There were three lines in the original version, but the first line was omitted by Genzo. The following is the original version:

1) *Shiki sei ze ku / ku sei ze shiki* (omitted)
2) *Shiki fu I ku / ku fu I shiki*
3) *Shiki soku ze ku / ku soku ze shiki*

Following the sequence, 1 leads to 2, which in turns leads to 3.

1) Emptiness is an aspect of form; form is an aspect of emptiness.
2) Form is not different from emptiness; emptiness is not different from form.
3) Form is the same as emptiness; emptiness is the same as form.

Lines two and three represent the worldview of a person who has actually experienced and attained enlightenment.

Line two, *Shiki fu I ku / ku fu I shiki* – implies impermanence, which is somewhat nihilistic.

Line three, *Shiki soku ze ku / ku soku ze shiki* – presents a positive view of the world.

To explain the relationship between form (body) and emptiness (mind):

1) The body is an aspect of the mind.
2) The body and mind, or the mind and body, are one and the same.
3) The body constitutes the mind; the mind constitutes the body.

Form is the same as emptiness; form is emptiness.
Emptiness is the same as form; emptiness is form.
(These lines are contradictory to *Shiki Soku Ze Ku*).

Form exists in emptiness. An empty state itself is form. When prajnaparamita is earnestly practiced in daily life, all visible objects will gradually vanish from view, leaving only emptiness behind. The body constitutes the mind, which is invisible and empty. (*Shiki Soku Ze Ku.*) Form and emptiness, i.e. substance and spirit, are both valuable; they cannot be treated as separate beings. Substance is made up of invisible particles. In its simplest form, matter is composed of particles, which are essentially empty. The visible world does not exist by itself; rather, the visible world consists of various interrelated elements. A material object cannot retain its shape forever. All physical phenomena are empty of substance. Everything happens according to the doctrine of dependent origination.

The body is the cause, the mind its effect. The mind causes the body to act. Action causes the five harmful elements to produce will. Will leads to experience, which in turn gives rise to intellect. Intellect causes the self to awaken. Everything is the result of the law of dependent origination. When the cause is eliminated, everything will cease to exist. Disappearance of the cause of suffering will result in the disappearance of suffering.

Ku Soku Ze Shiki is the opposite of *Shiki Soku Ze Ku*. As invisible particles in *ku* interact with each other, *shiki*, or visible objects will emerge. Nothing in this world is meaningless. The world is composed of interconnected elements.

Shiki Soku Ze Ku – Cause
Ku Soku Ze Shiki – Effect

    Form – Cause
    Emptiness – Cause
    Emptiness – Effect
    Form – Effect

This is the doctrine of dependent origination preached by the Buddha. Samsara is a term that describes the everlasting cycle of cause and effect. Funakoshi Gichin's *Karate-do* and Zen Buddhism both regard the state of *ku* expounded in the Heart Sutra as the supreme goal. Everything in the world is empty. Emptiness makes it possible for things to change into various forms. *Ku* and the self are united. *Ku* is devoid of substance, and so is the self. The self exists in nothingness that cannot be found anywhere. You will enjoy complete freedom when you transcend the material world. This is the only way you can experience absolute tranquility and joy in life.

The vast universe called *ku* makes human life possible. *Mu* (nothingness) is a projection of *ku*'s consciousness in the natural world. *Mu* signifies freedom of mind as well as *shin-myo-ryoku* (superhuman *waza*), which is free from attachment. Thought that arises in our mind gives rise to desire and attachment. To eliminate attachment, thought must be dispelled from our mind. Dispelling thought, the cause of suffering, allows you to return to the origin, where your mind is not restrained by attachment. The ultimate goal of *karate-do* is to reach a state of nothingness, when *shin-myo-ryoku* can be fully utilized. To obtain a real insight into the nature of *ku*, desire and attachment must be discarded.

When you see something beautiful, recognize its beauty without being attached to it; when you see something beautiful, acknowledge its beauty without being obsessed with it. The joy of life lies in *soku*.

8. *ZU SOU GYO SHIKI YAKU FUKU NYU ZE*
Likewise, sensation, representation (expression), will, and knowledge are all empty of substance.

Observing the nature of reality with the aid of prajnaparamita, he recognized the emptiness of sensation, expression, will, and knowledge.

9. *SHA RI SHI*
(Hear) Sariputra

10. *ZE SHO HO KU SO*
Various physical phenomena are manifestation of truth.

Being devoid of substance, *ku* is invisible. To understand the truth of *ku* is to understand the invisible truth. *Shiki* (form) is a reflection of *ku* (emptiness). When the mind's eye is open, you will be able to perceive this invisible realm and see through the mind of your opponent.

11. *FU SHO FU METSU*

Nothing is born or destroyed. (Nothing appears or disappears. No birth or death.)

An eternal life is not subject to birth or death, for it is never born or destroyed. *Ku* denotes an everlasting realm without a beginning or end. Everything in the natural world is transient. This life is so precious because we live only once. Immortality will be conferred upon those who live their life to the fullest. *Ku* must be thoroughly understood to attain eternal tranquility; *ku* must be experienced personally to know the meaning of life and death. The truth of *fu sho fu metsu* can be appreciated only when the fear of birth and death is overcome.

12. *FU KU FU ZYO*

No filthiness or impurity. (In *ku*, no one's reputation is tarnished by wrongdoing. No one repents his mistakes.)

Fu ku fu zyo refers to desire. One must transcend one's desire to attain enlightenment. Any inquiry into the origin of desire will eventually arrive at *ku*. In *ku*, desire is nonexistent. Even something that may appear filthy has a beautiful quality. Beauty in the true sense of the word has no desire. Ultimately, only a beautiful realm permeated with compassion really exists. The mind is useless if it is not pure. Genuine compassion means to embrace someone's pain as our own. Purity entails dirty elements; likewise, impurity always entails clean elements. Everything that exists in the world is neither pure nor impure.

13. *FU ZO FU METSU*

No increasing or decreasing. (Nothing increases or decreases. No gain or loss.)

Ideas about increasing or deceasing arise from our own judgment.

In the absence of human judgment, nothing really increases or decreases. What ultimately exists is an immutable and eternal world. The world of *ku* is everlasting and unchanging.

The three lines below describe the world of *ku* by negating the existence of the six elements:

(11) *Fu Sho Fu Metsu*

(12) *Fu Ku Fu Zyo*

(13) *Fu Zo Fu Metsu*

What they indicate is that there is no birth, destruction, filth, purity, increase or decrease in the world of *ku*.

14. *ZE KO KU CHU MU SHIKI*

To state it correctly, *shiki* does not exist in *ku*.

Thanks to the absence of form, the realm of emptiness can be known. The world of *ku* is insubstantial, inherently different from the world of *shiki* that is perceived through the eighteen dhatus or elements. The eighteen dhatus refer to *roku-shiki* (six forms of consciousness), *roku-kon* (six sense organs), and *roku-kyo* (objects of the six sense organs. *Roku-shiki* includes sight, hearing, smell, taste, touch, and intellect; *roku-kon* includes eyes, ears, nose, tongue, body, and mind; *roku-kyo* includes form, voice, scent, flavor, contact, and law (truth). No material objects or phenomena are present in *ku*, this, the eighteen dhatus are absent in *ku*.

15. *MU ZIU SO BYO SHIKI*

No sensation, expression, will, or knowledge.

The world of *ku* differs from the world that is perceived through the five organs. The five skandhas (body, sensation, expression, will, and knowledge) are necessary for human existence. The law of dependent origination is an inevitable outcome of the interaction of the five skandhas. Even the five skandhas are nonexistent in *ku*.

The Heart Sutra teaches that appearance does not necessarily translate into real existence.

Karate-do techniques involving sensation, expression, will, and knowledge will be empty once attachment is discarded. This will lead to *mu* (nothingness), a reflection of *ku* in the realm of consciousness. To reach a state of *mu*, attachment must be expelled from one's mind. *Shin-myo-ryoku*, or superhuman *waza*, will be possible only when your preoccupation with your skill and mind is abandoned. Realization of *mu* requires renunciation of attachment and self-discipline. Expanding one's self to the point where it becomes empty and nothing will open a gate to the realm of *ku* and *karate-do*.

16. *MU GEN NI BI ZE SHIN I*

Roku-kon refers to eyes, ears, nose, tongue, body and mind. *Kon* denotes an ability or organ.

No eye, nose, ear, tongue, body, or mind. The six sense organs, or *roku-kon*, do not exist in *ku*.

17. *MU SHIKI SHO KOU MI SOKU HO*

Roku-kyo refers to form, voice, scent, flavor, contact, and law.

No form, voice, sent, flavor, contact, or truth. The objects of the six sense organs, or *roku-kyo*, are absent in *ku*.

18. *MU GEN KAI / NAI SHI MU I SHI KAI*

Ku is eternally immutable. *Ku* represents a world without limit or attachment, encompassing everything from the visible realm to the realm of consciousness.

19. *MU MU MYO / YAKU MU MU MIYO ZIN*

No origin of suffering or misfortune. No ending of the origin of suffering or misfortune.

Human experience arises from *mu-myo*, which is the origin of suffering and misfortune. *Mu-myo* refers to illusory, mistaken wisdom. Instincts are part of *mu-myo*. The Buddha learned that it was *mu-myo* that caused life to emerge in a mother's womb. With this knowledge, he found a prescription for cessation of *mu-myo*. The Buddha traced back the sequence of human transformation and examined the flow of time from the past to the present and future. This eventually led him to the twelve links of dependent origination (*innen*, *engi*, or *hensen*). The Four Noble Truths (suffering, accumulation, extinction, and path), which are central to Buddhism, represent the Buddha's solution. He realized that a lack of prajnaparamita brought about suffering. When there is no desire, there will be no suffering. How can we put an end to suffering? The Buddha's answer was clear: practice and action. No enlightenment or illusion. No ending of enlightenment or illusion. For those who are unaware of illusion, enlightenment is not necessary. There is no need for them to seek enlightenment. You search for enlightenment because you are aware of illusion.

20. *NAI SHI MU ROU SHI / YAKU MU ROU SHI ZIN*
No aging or death. No termination of aging or death.

To live life to the fullest, you must keep your self-esteem high even during difficult times and free yourself from the fear of old age and death. Your heart will shine after many years of polishing; it will shine even more brilliantly with aging, symbolizing the fruit of your effort. Those in quests for *ku* must live, work hard, and appreciate the preciousness of life while they are alive, without fearing or seeking death.

Illusion and suffering lead to *sei-ro-byo-shi* (birth, old age, sickness, and death), which in turn leads to illusion and suffering. Unless *mu-myo* (ignorance) is eradicated, suffering and illusion will exist ceaselessly. When the fear of old age and death is overcome, the mind will glow beautifully, allowing one to live life to its fullest. *Ku* represents freedom. Once you understand this, you can solve any problem. *San-shien-ho* holds the three elements of *mu-myo*, love, and suffering are all interrelated. At the root of *engi/innen* (dependent origination) is love. Love is the origin of *mu-myo*. *Mu-myo* signifies a lack of understanding of prajnaparamita. Cessation of *mu-myo* results in cessation of love and suffering. This is the thrust of the doctrine of dependent origination, from which the concept of *ku* evolved.

The Buddha, after tracing back the sequence of human transformation and analyzing the flow of time from the past to the present and future, discovered a method of liberation from the bondage to suffering. What he found was the doctrine of dependent origination and the Four Noble Truths, which represent the Buddha's solution. These are the key concepts of Buddhism. Bear in mind that the absence of illusion does not necessarily mean enlightenment. Do not be confused about this point.

The twelve links of dependent origination (*innen/hensen/engi*)

Having discerned the chain of human transformation and unraveled the mystery of time from the past to the present and future, the Buddha discovered a method and a way of eradicating the cause of suffering. The twelve links of dependent origination are discussed below, with accompanying commentaries based on modern psychology. (Refer to Freudian or Jungian psychology.)

(1) *Mu-Myo* (Ignorance)

The cause of suffering lies in *mu-myo*. Suffering and illusion result when you are unaware of truth and the consequences of past desires. *Mu-myo* refers to ignorance that endlessly perpetuates the cycle of suffering.

Mu-myo

(2) *Gyo* (Action)

A new life is conceived through sexual intercourse. Not knowing truth, the seeds of suffering are planted and evil deeds involving conduct, speech and thought are perpetrated. Good and bad karma in the past produce certain consequences, determining the present condition of one's self.

(3) *Shiki* (Consciousness)

Consciousness begins to form in the womb of a mother. Shiki refers to the body and spirit that first emerge in the womb. *Roku-shiki* (eye, nose, ear, tongue, body, and mind) is the origin of suffering. Conception occurs as a result of past karma.

(4) *Myo-Shiki* (Name and Form)

The five body parts and six sense organs start growing inside the womb. This period begins after the fifth week of pregnancy and lasts until delivery. The faculties of *roku-kon* (eyes, nose, ear, tongue, and mind) are the source of suffering. *Myo-shiki* refers to the mind and body that develop inside the womb.

(5) *Roku-sho* (Development of the Six Sense Organs)

The five body parts and six sense organs are now fully developed. The fetus is about to leave the womb. The five body parts and six senses give rise to suffering.

(6) *Soku* (Contact)

Suffering results from the interaction of *roku-kon*, *roku-kyo*, and *roku-shiki*. The newborn baby still does not possess the sense of touch (warmness and coldness are indistinguishable to the infant). During this period, which lasts for three years after birth, cognitive processes are absent. This is considered a critical period in child development. An infant's psychological development is largely determined by how the mother breastfeeds and interacts with the child. Excessive scolding raises the levels of nor-adrenalin in an infant's body, making the child unmotivated and dependent. On the other hand, excessive praising elevates the levels of dopamine, making the child selfish and disobedient.

When a mother refuses to hold her infant and does not pay attention to the child even if he is crying, the infant is likely to believe that he is not worthy of love. In contrast, when a mother holds her infant often, protects him from danger, speaks to him constantly, and keeps him clean, the child is likely to feel that he is loved and well taken care of. *Soku* is the cause of suffering.

(7) *Ju* (Sensation)

Sensations produced in the mind bring about suffering. Children between five or six to thirteen or fourteen can experience simple sensations such as pain and pleasure. A child forms attachment to the objects of his craving. Four types of ability are underdeveloped in children under the age of five: inability to monitor reality, lack of the "magic number" ability, inability to grasp the concept of time, underdevelopment of the ability to anticipate. Each of these can give rise to suffering.

Inability to monitor reality means that the capacity to distinguish one thing from another is underdeveloped. For instance, a child may confuse reality with imagination, fantasy, wish, and imitation.

The magic number refers to the number of items a person can memorize for a short period of time. Adults can memorize up to seven items at once (in other words, the magic number is seven). For children under five, one's age minus one is their magic number. Children younger than five can clearly remember daily events and their impressions of those events, but are unable to memorize a large number of items at once. Such children only talk about the things they can remember, but are unaware that they are omitting some details.

When the ability to anticipate is underdeveloped, you cannot foresee whether the other person will believe your statement. Children tell lies in an attempt to avoid a scolding, but their parents can easily detect their lies. Young children under five years of age tell lies, but their lies are too obvious and should not be taken seriously. As the ability to anticipate develops, children will tell fewer lies.

The ability to grasp the concept of time refers to the mental capacity to track the flow of time from the past to the present and future. Children younger than five lack this ability.

When children are about four years old, their lies become more elaborate. Lies during this period are necessary for children to establish personal relationships as well as to acquire social skills. Since children are unaware of their own lies at this stage, adults should not admonish children for their lies without giving them a chance to explain. Adults need to make sure that children know what prompted them to lie. Children are likely to admit lying when they are asked to remember what motivated them to lie. Even if children cannot remember anything, adults should not scold them. Do not cross-question children. Try to understand their feelings and help them clarify their thoughts. When children older than five tell lies, they must be reproached. However, it is important to raise the spirits of children after they are admonished. Otherwise, children will continue to tell lies whenever something inconvenient happens. By cheering up children after a scolding, adults can earn their trust. As a result, such children are more likely to honestly admit lying.

The age group between three and seven represents the first rebellious period. Children in this age group begin to show sexual desire and interest in genitals. A boy turns his attention to his mother and grows jealous of his father. Despite the boy's hatred for his father, the father becomes the object of his adoration. Hatred can turn into terror, and the boy may react to his father's anger with anxiety. The boy attempts to break free from his father's influence while accepting the presence of his father. Through this process, he enters a new stage, during which his ego is awakened. At this rebellious stage, children feel both love and hatred for their parents.

Jealousy prompts a girl to direct her hatred toward the mother. As the girl becomes conscious of her fathers emotions, feminine sensibility will develop in her. All of the above can give rise to suffering.

(8) *Ai* (love)

Fundamental desire to avoid pain and seek pleasure. Attachment to desire leads to suffering. *Ai* arises in children older than fourteen. At this stage, children become attached to desire for wealth and affection. Children over seven up to puberty repress their sexual urges and enter a dormant period.

(9) *Shu* (Grasping)

Desire for possession causes suffering. The period from adolescence to young adulthood represents a time of confusion about one's sexual desire. During this stage, the inner conflict young adults had experienced in their childhood returns. Their sexual desire is being integrated at this stage. When a boy begins to rebel against his father, the father must provide emotional support for his son.

If the father is unsupportive, his son will be puzzled and confused. Through such confrontation, the boy gets to know his father, eventually identifying with him. He may develop a defiant attitude. The boy's defiant attitude does not have to be directed at his father; the target can be a powerful figure or a monster in a dream. Such confrontation is necessary for the young man to learn how to control his emotions. Without this experience, the boy may become fearful of a father figure, develop neurosis, be easily intimidated by a person in authority, or have a tendency to become tense and confused.

A girl awakens to her own sexuality. She begins to feel hatred and envy for men. Inwardly, she resents the fact that she was not born a boy.

When this resentment turns into inferiority complex, she may react or act aggressively toward men. Young women should accept their female sexuality during this period; otherwise, they may become overly masculine, making it difficult to obtain sexual satisfaction.

As the father begins to recognize the feminine qualities of his daughter, the girl becomes conscious of his presence. She beings to engage in direct dialogue with her mind. The father's strength helps his daughter to develop feminine sensitivity and sensibility. A girl with an effeminate father cannot properly develop female sensitivity, and as a result, may become unwomanly. When the father is more permissive with his daughter than the mother, the girl is likely to reach puberty without experiencing the father's masculine qualities. All of the above can be a source of suffering.

(10) *U* (Becoming)
Past karma created by *ai* and *shu* have inevitable consequences. When there is a cause of suffering, there will be suffering. *Ai* and *shu* shape the course of this life, which in turn determines the course of the next life. Desire to possess the origin of desire begins about suffering.

(11) *Sei* (Life)
Sei perpetuates the cycle of human existence. Life comes from desire for love. Life is the cause of suffering. This life will spawn another life in the future.

(12) *Rou-sei* (Aging)
Life entails death. It is painful to grow old and face death. Old age and death will continue to beset us in our next life.

21. *MU KU SHU METSU DO*
No *ku-shu-metsu-do* (suffering, accumulation, extinction, path). *Shi-tai* (The Four Noble Truths) does not exist in ku.

Shi-tai consists of *ku* (suffering), *shu* (accumulation), *metsu* (extinction), and *do* (path). *Tai* denotes the ability to discern the true nature of reality. *Shi-tai* refers to four truths. These four truths symbolize the Buddha's enlightenment. Even *shi-tai* is absent in *ku*. The Heart Sutra reflects the

Buddha's mind. It was *shi-tai* and the doctrine of dependent origination that the Buddha preached for 45 years after his enlightenment until his death. These four truths are as follows:

(1) *Ku-tai*

The human ego is formed in parallel with the development of the mind and body. This is the origin of suffering. Suffering occurs when one is unable to have full control of a situation or possess the objects of desire. A living being is always tormented by unsatisfied desire. Life is the beginning of suffering.

Ignorance causes suffering. Old age and death cause suffering. Being unable to satisfy one's craving causes suffering. Having to deal with people you do not get along with or those you bear a grudge against and detest causes suffering. Attachment causes suffering. Suffering can be your best friend as well as your worst enemy. Self-discipline, self-examination, and self-effort can greatly reduce suffering.

(2) *Jit-tai*

Accumulation of sources of suffering leads to suffering. The origin of suffering is attachment. Once the cause of suffering is identified, a method of terminating suffering can be found.

(3) *Met-tai*

Removal of attachment can eliminate and extinguish suffering.

(4) *Do-tai*

The Eight-Fold Path. Eight Right Paths. We must follow the middle path and modify our behavior in accordance with the Eightfold path.
* Right Judgment (being able to see the ultimate reality)
* Right Thought
* Right Expression (being able to speak the truth)
* Right Action and Work
* Right Living
* Right Effort
* Right Contemplation
* Right Understanding

The right path is the middle path without extremes. We must practice the middle path without being attached to extremes. *Ku* is the middle path; the middle path is *ku*. By transcending the Four Noble Truths, we can elevate our thoughts and understand the concept of *ku*.

[Translation and Commentary]
The five body parts and six senses are at the root of suffering. Removal of the cause of suffering leads to elimination of attachment. Termination of suffering requires knowledge and adherence to the Four Noble Truths. However, *ku* does not even contain the Four Noble Truths.

22. *MU CHI YAKU MU TOKU / I MU SHO TOKO KO*
No wisdom or attainment; nothing is attained in *ku*.

Mu Chi Yaku Mu Toku – No wisdom or attainment. *Toku* denotes enlightenment. There is nothing beneficial or virtuous in *ku*.

I Mu Sho Toku Ko – *Mu Sho Toku* refers to innocence and purity of mind, which enable us to achieve our ultimate goal. *I mu sho toku ko* means non-attainment. No one is enlightened; no one has been enlightened. When there is no attainment, attachment will never arise. With nothing to be attained, illusion and suffering will soon dissipate. The Heart Sutra elucidates the principle of *ku*. The following lines explain how the principle of *ku* should be interpreted.

23. *BO DAI SAT TA*
Bo dai sat ta is a spiritually awakened person, a person who has opened his eyes to the truth of *ku*. He is an awakened being who strives to awaken others. Those aspiring to reach this stage should abandon their greed and practice compassion.

24. *E HAN NYA HA RA MIT TA KO*
Because Bo-dai-sat-ta has attained prajnaparamita…

25. *SHIN MU KEI GE*
Nothing interrupts or impedes his mind.

26. *MU KEI GE KO*

Because nothing impedes his mind... *mu kei ge* means that the mind is completely liberated from worry and concern.

27. *MU U KU FU*

Fearless. Fear denotes feelings of trepidation and terror. Fear comes from lack of wisdom. A fearful person is overly conscious of his enemies and is easily frightened by their shadows. A Zen practitioner devotes all his energies to live in the moment. He lives his life without worrying about the future.

Note for lines twenty-three through twenty-seven: Having realized prajnaparamita, Bo-dai-sat-ta has no fear in his mind. Nothing interrupts or impedes his mind. Because nothing impedes his mind, he is fearless.

28. *ON RI IT SAI TEN DO MU SO*

With distracting thoughts dispelled... *on ri* means to be detached from distracting thoughts. *Ten do mu so* refers to distracting ideas or delusion that emerge in the confused mind. There are four types of *ten do mu so*: the delusion that one will live forever (this delusion derives from one's attachment to life and death), the delusion that life is pleasurable (ignorance of the that that life is suffering), the delusion that one's self really exists, the delusion that the body is pure (this delusion stems from one's attachment to the impure body). These delusions result when you turn your eyes away from truth.

29. *KU KYO NE HAN*

A state of peace without attachment. Detachment and absolute freedom are attained. *Nehan* represents an ideal state as well as our supreme goal. With distractions and attachment completely removed, eternal tranquility is realized. *Ne Han* (nirvana) denotes the absence of creation and destruction. It means to extinguish the flames of desire. It is a real where quietness prevails. After attaining every virtue and dispelling illusion from the mind, one enters nirvana, a state of absolute tranquility. The ultimate goal of life is to enrich life. To enrich life, one must gain a true insight into the nature of nirvana. Being devoid of substance, *ku* has no objects of conflict or attachment. This is why the mind is at peace in *ku*.

Certain training is necessary to attain enlightenment. There are three training methods. The objective of each training method is to realize our ideals.

1. *Shi-tai* (suffering, accumulation, extinction, path)
2. Twelve links of *innen* (dependent origination)
3. Six paramitas (*huse, ji-kai, nin-niku, syo-jin, zen-jo, chie*)
   - *Huse* or *dana* (giving) – There are two types of donation: donation intended to dispel someone's fear and donation intended to make someone feel relieved. Offerings should not be given with selfish motives. Acceptance of offerings by a recipient diminishes the donor's materialistic desires. A donor, recipient, and gift must be empty and pure.
   - *Ji-kai* or *sila* (morality) – Observance of the precepts (this should be done spontaneously).
   - *Nin-niku* or *ksanti* (patience) – To endure embarrassment and oppression. To restrain one's anger and remain calm.
   - *Sho-jin* or *virya* (diligence) – Completion of the right path through self-effort.
   - *Zen-jo* or *dhyana* (meditation) – To practice meditation and rectify one's mind in accordance with the Eightfold path.
   - *Chie* or *prajna* (wisdom) – To observe the ultimate nature of reality. To attain true wisdom.

30. *SAN ZE SHO BUTSU*

This refers to buddhas with a complete understanding of the past, present, and future.

31. *E HAN NYA HA RA MIT TA KO*

Thanks to a thorough understanding of prajnaparamita, buddhas have acquired *toku a noku ta ra san miyaku san bo dai*. Note: Having understood the empty nature of the world, Buddha became a savior filled with compassion, who strove to relieve the suffering of others.

32. *TOKU A NOKU TA RA SAN MIYAKU SAN BO DAII*

Owing to a thorough understanding of prajnaparamita, buddhas of the past, present, and future have attained supreme enlightenment, which is infinitely great, right, and universal. *A noku ta ra* mean supreme. *San Miyaku* means right.

To attain the highest wisdom is to attain prajnaparamita. Prajna-paramita is infinitely great, right, and universal. The recognition that the pursuit of truth has no limit or end will make you feel humble. Once you realize this you will study and train with humility. Through train-ing, you will enter the mind of the Buddha, eventually becoming one with the Buddha himself. This is the greatest enlightenment.

33. *KO CHI HAN NITA HA RA MIT TA*

Prajnaparamita itself is a magnificent mantra.

34. *ZE DAI ZIN SHU*

This is a mantra with the power to conquer evil.

35. *ZE DAI MYO SHU*

This is a mantra that uncovers perfect wisdom.

36. *ZE MU ZYO SHU*

This is the supreme mantra.

37. *ZE MU TO DO SHU*

This is the unparalleled mantra. These four lines indicate that this great-est and unequaled mantra possesses mystical powers.

38. *NO ZYO IT SAI KU*

This mantra can eradicate all suffering.

39. *SHIN ZI TSU HO KO KO*

This mantra is not untrue or false. Truth is synonymous with God. Truth cannot be expressed, perceived, or experienced. It can only be known empirically through spiritual cultivation. Truth is revealed only momentarily. The secrets of the martial arts are revealed in the same way. What are the secrets of the martial arts? It is to be able to discern the presence of eternal life and to experience *ku* (emptiness) and *mu* (nothingness). A person's viewpoint cannot be changed overnight. Bear in mind that training is necessary to develop the ability to observe the world from the perspective of *ku* and *engi* (dependent origination). Some practitioners of Buddhism and the martial arts lose sight of truth when they become knowledgeable. This happens because of attachment. In the martial arts, such people are said to have a poor mental attitude. It is important to act naturally and spontaneously. For instance, we should rejoice in times of joy and cry in times of sorrow. However, we should not be preoccupied with or tormented by our emotions. When tormented by our emotions, our mobility will be impaired, making it difficult to see other things clearly. Nothing is more unreliable in our mind. Oftentimes, our life is dictated by desire that originates in our mind.

Everything in the world is perceived through the mind. Good and evil are merely concepts that are created by our mind. The human mind is intrinsically pure. To be enlightened is to restore purity of mind. In *ku*, truth is revealed only fleetingly.

40. *KO SETSU HAN NYA HA RA MIT TA SHU*
Prajnaparamita. Merely reciting the sutra will not suffice. Confirm the authenticity of this perfect wisdom with your heart and translate it into action. The mantra that actualizes prajnaparamita should now be proclaimed. At this stage, one is returning from a state of enlightenment, after obtaining a true insight into the nature of *ku*; completion of enlightenment is only one step away. *Han niya ha ram it ta* is a magnificent mantra. This incomparable mantra has the power to end all suffering. The mantra is recited in the following way.

41. *SOKU SETSU SHU WAKU*
The mantra is recited in the following way.

42. *GYA TEI GYA TEI*
An awakened being, awakened being (enlightened one, enlightened one). To those who have comprehended the Four Noble Truths and

attained *ku*, congratulations on your success. Let's strive to achieve perfect enlightenment, our ultimate goal.

The first *gya tei* refers to those who have attained enlightenment by following the advice of their mentors, whereas the second refers to those who have become enlightened through self-effort.

Gya-tei

43. *HA RA GYA TEI*

It is time to awaken others to the truth. (This line indicates that various buddhas' efforts have finally come to fruition.)

Now that you have grasped the meaning of *ku* and have been liberated from the concepts of *ku* and *mu*, it is time to translate prajnaparamita you have acquired into action in your daily life. At this final state of enlightenment, it is your duty to engage in charitable activities that will benefit society and assist others in attaining enlightenment. Completion of enlightenment is near. Achieving your own enlightenment will not suffice; others must be awakened to the truth as well. There is no difference between your happiness and someone else's happiness. Someone else's happiness is your happiness. Guide others to their enlightenment by removing attachment from their minds. By so doing, your enlightenment will be fully attained. No matter what happens—in difficult, happy, or sad times, or on a rainy, stormy, or sunny day—you must steadfastly practice prajnaparamita in your daily life, without being distracted by worldly matters. Discard your obsession with *ku* and follow the middle path by avoiding the extremes of right and left. Be a spiritual guide for others. This is the only way you can attain perfect enlightenment.

Gya tei gya tei ha ra gya tei refers to the final state of enlightenment. At this stage, one must assiduously practice prajnaparamita in one's daily life without being attached to *ku* and *mu*. Supreme awakening will be realized by engaging in charitable activities, guiding others to the realm of *ku*, and awakening them to the truth.

44. *HA RA SO GYA TEI*

Oh, bhiksu and bhiksuni. Having reached a state of *ku* and *mu*, you are now liberated from *ku* and *mu*. Enter the final phase of prajnaparamita to approach the Buddha's mind. (Note: Each individual's efforts to comprehend the mantra have come to fruition.)

45. *BO JI SO WA KA*

Let us achieve supreme enlightenment.

The ultimate purpose of enlightenment is indicated here. This line is a congratulatory remark for those who have reached a state of *ku* by practicing prajnaparamita and transcending desire. Up until this point, everything has been negated. Finally, absolute affirmation is expressed here with the repetition of *gya tei*. Attaining your enlightenment is not enough; you must help others awaken to the truth. Someone's happiness translates into your happiness. This is the only way you can attain perfect enlightenment. Prajnaparamita is now realized.

46. *HAN NIYA SHIN GYO*

How to contemplate and act to realize prajnaparamita (how to contemplate and act to enter the mind of the Buddha).

AFTERWORD

The world of martial arts is profound.

The main goal of this book was to explain the spiritual aspects of martial arts and how we can put this knowledge to practical use. In order to achieve that goal, the following questions had to be addressed:

What do we need to learn?

What is the mind?

What is the body?

What is technique?

What is the art of tactics?

What is spirituality? In my search for answers, I delved deeper into the realm of spiritual enlightenment our predecessors had shed light on in the past.

ACKNOWLEDGMENTS

I would like to express my deepest gratitude to the following individuals for their assistance in the creation of this book: Keiichi Hasumi Sensei, who kindly took the trouble to write a foreword to this book, my teacher Hisao Obata Sensei for his support and encouragement, and my great friends Katsuhiko Maruoka and Kyozi Kasao Senpai, who gave me valuable advice.

I am immensely grateful to Tom Shea, Jeremy Chassen, Deb Chassen, Jared Chassen, Kanae Koh, Popsi Narasimhan, Melissa Briscoe, Zinger Yang, Arthur Kerr, Paget Wharton, Debra Martinez, Malte Loos, Billy Conigliaro, and Arielle Chassen for taking the time out of their busy schedule to edit the manuscript of this book.

Special thanks to the following translators who demonstrated their outstanding ability: Junko Kamei and Maiko Hirai of Mechie, Yumiko Fukumoto, Momoko Kawaguchi, Eriko Kobayashi, Yoko Masuki, Yukiko Nishizake, Natsuki Oka, Rieko Russell, Tomomo Maekawa, Mr. & Mrs. Kasu Kaede Uji, Tomomi Aozono, Jiroshi Minato, Tse Hwanyong, Hiromi Kumasaki, and Shinya Yamada. Your help is truly appreciated.

I am also deeply indebted to the following organization for all their support: The New England Collegiate Karate Conference, the NAKF, and Bermuda Tabata-Ha Shotokan.

REFERENCES AND ORIGINAL CITATIONS

Takefuru Sakuragi. *Dokyowotukeruhon.* S. 52. Parusushupan KK.

Tsugita Masaki. 1980. *Koziki.* Kodansha.

Kanaya Osamu. 1994. *Kanbishi.* Iwanmishoten.

Uzita Tsutomo. 1988. *Niponshoki.* Kodansha

Noshio Minoru, Nogami Toyoichro. *Fushikaden.* Iwanamishoten.

Yuki Aoki. 1995. *Zeni No Ningengaku.* KK Robgusera-zu.

Mikyo Nosuke. 1976. *Keieisha-no-joken.* PHP Kenkyujo.

Kawade Shoboshinsha, Hachiya Kunio. 1996. *ChuGoku Shisotowa.* Nandarowka.

Muramatsu Ei. *Chugoku Sansennen No Taishitsu.* S.55. Takagisho Bo.

Yasuoka Masahiro. 1997. *Mo-shi.* Mokudehan.K.K.

Yasuoka Masahiro. 2005. *Jiuhachi-Shiryaku.* PHP Ken Kyuzyuo.

Moriya Hiroshi. 1977. *Shokatsu Komei No Heho.* Tokuma Shoten.

Riri Furanku. 1998, *Daremoshiranai Meigen Shu.* Jo Ho Senter Shupan Kyoku.

Nakamura Hajime. 2003. *Hannya Kyoten.* Tokyo Shoseki KK.

Nakamura Hajime. 2003. *Kegonkyo Ryogakyo.* Tokyo Shosei KK.

Nakamura Hajime. 2003. *Uimakyo Shoman Gyo.* Tokyo Shosei KK.

Nakamura Hajime. 2004. *Ronsho Hoka.* Tokyo Shosei KK.

Nakamura Hajime. 2003. *Jyo Do Kyo Ten.* Tokyo Shosei KK.

Nakamura Hajime. 2003. *Hokekyo.* Tokyo Shosei KK.

Nakamura Hajime. 2004. *Mitkyokyoten Hoka.* Tokyo Shosei KK.

Sai-do-Parishu-Sa-Batshu. 2002. *Hiden Nipon Budo Igaku.* Fukushodo.

Murayama Makoto. 1996. *Sonshi Goshi.* Tokumashoten.

Moriya Hiroshi I. 1999. *Sonshi Goshi.* KK Purejidentosha.

Moriya Hiroshi. 1999. *Shibaho Utsuryoshi Rieikomontai.* KK Purejidentosha.

Nicholas A. Chistrakis. 1999. *Death Foretold.* University of Chicago.

Wanabe Sho. 1969. *Kao Karada Teso Ni Yoru Jikoshindan.* Kowado.

Tago Akira. *Bukaoshikaru Shinrigijutu.* Gomashobo.

Hayazima Masao. *Wakasagayomigaeru Do In Zutu Nyumon.* S.57 Gomashobo.

Harai Tomio. *Zazen Kenko Ho.* S.49. Otomashobo.

Serizawa Katsuhiko. *Zintaitsubo No Kenkyu.* Gomashobo.

Asano Hachiro. *Soseiuranai.* Kobunsha.

D. Ka Negi, (Yaku) Yamaguchi Hiroshi. *Hitowo Ugokasu.* S.33. Sogensha.

Hariyama Akira. Michiwahirakeru. S.34. Sogensha.

Murayama Makoto. 1987. *Hitowougokasu Is No Gokui.* Misakashobo.

Oohashi Takeo. *Heiho De Kaiei Suru.* S.52. Bizinesusha.

Kamada Hasaru. *Bukawomottarayumuhon.* S.52. Nipon Zitu Gyoshupansha.

Dr. Thomas Gordon, Kondo Tako (Yaku). 1977. *Ri Da Kunren Ho.* Naimaru Shupankai.

Hamuro Yoriaki. 1997. *Shindo No Kokoro.* Shunshusya.

Shotokan Karate Magazine. October 2006. SKM Publications.